Patio & Stone

A *Sunset* Design Guide

by Tom Wilhite and the editors of Sunset Books

Contents

A beautiful landscape is more than just a collection of plants—structure is needed to create inviting outdoor spaces. An appealing and comfortable patio lures you outside, whether it's a simple paved area with a couple of chairs or an elaborate outdoor room that includes a kitchen or even a pool. For patios and other "hardscape" elements like paths, garden walls, raised beds, and water features, there is no better material to use than stone. With its natural simplicity and unmatched durability, stone has a timeless appeal.

In these pages, you'll find a wealth of ideas for handsome garden features made from rock-hard materials, along with design tips from a panel of experts on creating great patios and using stone effectively in the landscape. From fire pits to ponds and pools, from suggestions for patio plants to tips on how to arrange boulders, you'll discover countless options to add to your own landscape.

6

112

Design Panel

The following design and landscaping professionals from across the United States lent their enormous talent and valuable advice to the pages of this book.

SUNSET BOOKS

Vice President, Editorial Director: Bob Doyle
Art Director: Vasken Guiragossian

STAFF FOR THIS BOOK

Senior Editor: Carrie Dodson Davis
Project Editor: Terri L. Robertson
Consulting Editor: Marianne Lipanovich
Principal Photographer: Michele Lee Willson
Principal Photo Stylist: Laura Del Fava
Copy Editor: Pam Cornelison
Proofreader: Denise Griffiths
Indexer: Marjorie Joy
Prepress Coordinators: Danielle Johnson and
Eligio Hernandez
Production: Precision Graphics
Intern: Shea Stakowski

Cover Photo: Photography by
Linda Lamb Peters

For additional copies of
Patio & Stone: A Sunset Design Guide
or any other Sunset book,
visit us at www.oxmoorhouse.com.
For more exciting home and garden ideas,
visit www.myhomeideas.com.

Baldassare Mineo
HORTICULTURIST

Baldassare Mineo moved in 1978 to Medford, Oregon, where he has pursued his love of plants as a nursery owner, horticulture expert, author, journalist, lecturer, botanical artist, and photographer. He owned and operated Siskiyou Rare Plant Nursery, an alpine- and rock-garden specialty nursery, for 27 years. These extraordinary plants continue to be his passion, although in his 2-acre, 30-year-old garden, he attempts to grow every cold-hardy plant under the sun. He is the author of the widely respected reference book, *Rock Garden Plants, A Color Encyclopedia.*

Cameron Scott
LANDSCAPE DESIGNER

Cameron Scott is the owner of Exteriorscapes, a full-service landscape design, construction, and maintenance firm in Seattle. His childhood passions for art and nature were nourished through studying oil painting and learning about plants alongside his gardener parents. He started a lawn service as a youth, worked his way through college as a landscaper, and studied landscape design in the Caribbean. He ultimately settled in Seattle, where he cofounded Exteriorscapes in 1994. Specializing in custom stone work, sustainable technologies, naturalistic gardens, and water management, the firm has grown steadily into one of the most innovative and respected in the Puget Sound area.
www.exteriorscapes.com

Craig Bergmann
LANDSCAPE ARCHITECT

Craig Bergmann Landscape Design (CBLD) was founded in 1986, and has four divisions: Design, Installation, Garden Care, and Nursery. Craig serves as Head of Design, working with a staff of 75 employees, including six designers. He is a registered landscape architect and frequent lecturer, and was recently featured as a nationwide speaker in *Horticulture* magazine's Nationwide Symposia Series. CBLD is noted for its modern-day twists on the romantic designs of the past. The company has received numerous awards, including Best of Show at several consecutive Chicago Flower & Garden Shows.
www.craigbergmann.com

Tara Dillard
GARDEN DESIGNER

Tara Dillard is a nationally recognized garden designer, author, and speaker, who has hosted her own television program, *The Better Gardening Show*. After earning degrees in engineering and horticulture, she began designing and installing low-maintenance organic landscapes more than 20 years ago—landscapes with an emphasis on the balance between home, garden, and life. An award-winning author of five books, including *Garden Paths and Stepping Stones, Beautiful by Design,* and *The Garden View,* Tara also writes a weekly newspaper column and maintains a popular blog on her website. Based in Atlanta, Georgia, she lectures nationally, spreading the message that creating a beautiful landscape will create a beautiful life.
www.taradillard.com

Scott Colombo
LANDSCAPE DESIGNER

Scott Colombo's passion for gardening was cultivated by his Italian grandmother's love of all things outdoors. With an educational background in landscape architecture and business management, he established his own design-and-build firm, Scott Colombo Designs. Some of his designs are boldly contemporary, while many others, influenced by his European travels, reveal a fondness for antique materials and rustic artifacts. He has a particular talent for creating garden spaces with the appearance of aged permanence. Scott's work has won numerous awards and has been featured in many publications over the past two decades, including *Sunset* magazine.
www.scottcolombodesigns.com

Jan Nielsen
STONE CONSULTANT

Jan Nielsen is the marketing and special projects manager for Marenakos Rock Center, a third-generation family-owned business near Seattle, and one of the oldest and largest stone suppliers in the Northwest. The trend toward using natural stone in landscape designs has kept Jan busy consulting on projects of all sizes, from mansions on the San Juan Islands to rooftop gardens atop Seattle condominiums. His work involves everything from consulting with sculptors on large urban installations to helping homeowners with placement of landscape stones in a local backyard. Through years of experience seeing projects through from quarry to installation, Jan has developed a special insight into the world of stone.
www.marenakos.com

Bernard Trainor
LANDSCAPE DESIGNER

Bernard Trainor practiced and studied landscape design in Australia and Europe before opening his firm, Bernard Trainor + Associates, in California's Monterey Bay area. Working in such different environments developed his ability to see each new project with fresh, inquisitive eyes. While the vernacular of each site may vary, he always strives to observe the genius of the place, connect with the architecture, and respond to the personality of the client. His stated goal is to design contextual outdoor spaces that engage and inspire people every day. Trainor's work has won numerous awards and has been widely featured in print, including a number of *Sunset* publications.
www.bernardtrainor.com

Karen Aitken
LANDSCAPE ARCHITECT

Karen Aitken has been designing gardens in Northern California for the past 30 years, and currently resides in Gilroy, California. She received her Bachelor of Science degree in landscape architecture from California Polytechnic State University, San Luis Obispo, and has been a registered California Landscape Architect since 1983. Her firm, Aitken & Associates, is known for creating thoughtful, innovative, and environmentally conscious landscapes throughout the region. In 2005, her exceptional design for Gilroy Gardens received an award for "Most Beautiful Theme Park in the West." A part-time resident of Baja California, Karen enjoys painting its landscapes and kayaking among the dolphins in the Sea of Cortez.
www.aitkenlandscapes.com

Chapter 1
Materials

Strength and durability are two obvious requirements when it comes to choosing materials for landscape features such as patios, paths, and garden walls. You also want your chosen material to add beauty to your property, both at installation time and after it's been subjected to the elements for a number of years. Natural stone is always a fine choice for hardscaping, but manmade materials can work beautifully too, depending on the site and budget. The intrinsic hardness of all of these materials is a perfect foil to the softness of plants and water. In this chapter, you can review the many hardscaping materials available for use in the garden.

Design Considerations

This colorful contemporary garden uses a variety of hardscape elements in varying elevations. Square concrete slabs set among blue-gray pebbles are surrounded by plants that soften the edges.

One of the first choices to make when you're planning a new patio, wall, or other landscape feature is which material to use. For structures that connect to the house, such as an adjoined patio, an entry stairway, or a raised bed outside the kitchen door, you'll want to give careful consideration to the architectural style of the house. To guarantee harmony, use materials of similar colors and textures to those of the house. You can also achieve a pleasing effect with contrast, but plan your choices carefully rather

than making them as you go. With structures detached or farther from the house—such as a patio tucked in a corner of the backyard or a streetside raised bed—you can be more flexible, using distance and plants as a sort of visual buffer.

Natural stone typically has a rough feel, though it can look very elegant when trimmed for use in paving or walls. Manmade materials can be used for a more contemporary effect: Consider the uniformity of a brick patio or a clean line of concrete pavers slicing across a river of lawn.

TOP RIGHT A stone bench designed as part of a retaining wall tucks into a bank of fragrant plants. It creates a cozy spot for sitting down or even stretching out.

RIGHT The color and texture of this flagstone path is in perfect harmony with its surroundings. Its semi-smooth surface complements both the rough texture of the boulders and the smooth surface of the stucco fence pillars.

Natural Stone

Natural stone gives a timeless look to any landscape feature, be it a flagstone patio, a dry-stacked wall made from small boulders, or a cobblestone edging for a garden path. Stone weathers beautifully too, often accumulating highlights of moss and lichen with the passing years. Most types of stone change color when wet, darkening and glistening when showered with rain or by sprinklers. Stone surfaces need little or no maintenance to keep their

good looks year-round. They provide visual interest in the landscape when surrounding plants are out of bloom or have gone dormant for the winter. And natural stone is extremely durable: A properly installed stonescape could last for hundreds of years.

In the following pages, you'll see the various forms in which natural stone is available, including everything from huge, rugged boulders you might stand on to river pebbles you might

scoop up to admire. Being products of nature, no two stones are exactly alike, so no two rock walls or pathways can look precisely the same. And most different types of stones will complement each other in the landscape. "In my opinion," says stone expert Jan Nielsen, "it is best to have different types of stone for the walls than you do for the flagstone; the contrast makes the spaces more interesting."

LEFT This Asian-inspired garden features an island of flat stone in a sea of gravel. A curving path of stone steps invites movement through the hillside.

TOP Looking as if they had simply tumbled into place, these good-sized boulders are ideal for a retaining wall. Rough steps of matching stone lead from a gravel patio to a rustic wooden bridge.

ABOVE A manmade waterfall and fern plantings create a beautiful hillside setting. Smooth stones mimic eons of erosion.

TOP LEFT Rough-textured flagstones with pebbles between them make a fine surface for a casual patio or pathway.

BOTTOM LEFT In perfect harmony with the color and style of the house, this entryway uses a variety of materials, including granite cobblestones and edging, precision-cut flagstones of slate, and veneer stone facing.

RIGHT What could be simpler or more effective than large, chunky flagstone stepping-stones leading through a lush garden? Boulders and smaller stones nearly concealed among the foliage include the same colors and texture of the flagstones.

Choosing Stone

When it comes to choosing natural stone for your landscape, there are so many choices: granite, basalt, limestone, sandstone, slate, marble, bluestone, just to name a few. You can study books like this one and use the Internet to explore the many options, but there is no substitute for seeing and touching the material itself. Plan a trip to a local stone yard

to discover the types of stone you find most appealing.

Stone from a local source is often the best choice for any project. It always looks right and somehow "fits," especially in the more natural parts of the garden. You might want to use more exotic stone for an area very near the house, such as a patio, where you step from an indoor tile floor to a cut-stone floor of a similar color outside. Local stone is usually the least expensive, because it costs less to transport from the quarry.

For the most natural look, limit your choices to just one or two types of stone, or at least look for harmonious colors. Stonescapes that include too many textures and colors look jumbled and can be disorienting.

Flagstones

Flagstones are large, flat slabs of stone that are generally 1 to 3 inches thick. Irregular in shape, they often have a slightly roughened surface that provides good traction when wet. Flagstones at least 1½ inches thick can be used for stepping-stones or as patio flooring laid directly in soil or on a sand bed. Thinner ones need to be laid in wet mortar or concrete to prevent cracking. Flagstone can also be stacked to make an attractive wall. It's available in a wide range of colors, from black slate to nearly white sandstone.

Cut Stone

Cut stone, sometimes called stone tile, is similar to flagstone, but it has been cut into square or rectangular shapes. This gives it a much more formal look than flagstones. The back of cut stone is always flat, and the edges are sawn. The top surface of the stone can be smooth or manipulated to have a variety of textures. Hammering, flaming, sandblasting, and tumbling are some of the processes used to create texture.

STONE CONSULTANT
JAN NIELSEN ON

Surface Texture

Since flagstone and cut stone are often used for flooring, you need to consider what activities will be taking place on the stone. "For instance, if this is for your front walkway, the surface should be as even as possible, and there may even be building code requirements to consider," Nielsen says. "In the backyard, you can be a little more creative with your choices, since friends and family will have some awareness of the layout. If furniture will be set on the stone, it needs to be flat and even, as a rocking table can be awfully hard on wineglasses."

OPPOSITE PAGE Large flagstones surrounded by a flowering ground cover are perfect for creating a small patio. Smaller flagstones were used to create an adjoining path for a seamless feel.

TOP A spacious, elegant entry patio features cut stone in a subtle palette of tan, gray, and beige that blends nicely with the brick wall and wooden furniture. The surface is nearly as smooth as indoor flooring.

BOTTOM An inlaid swirl of cut stone in descending sizes brings a stylish new dimension to a patio floor of close-set flagstone.

Cobblestones

Cobblestones were used to pave early streets. They were originally rounded stones up to 10 inches in diameter that were gathered from local streams and rivers and laid close together on a bed of sand or mortar. Later, the more familiar square-edged cobblestones came into use. Usually carved from granite into 4- to 5-inch cubes or shaped like large bricks up to 12 inches long, the cobblestones available today are either cut by the stone yard or reclaimed from an old street.

Because of their size, cobblestones are easy to work with. They rarely need cutting to fit into a given space. They work best when wedged fairly tightly together. You can create interesting patterns by laying square and rectangular ones together. A cobblestone path adds an antique look to the landscape. Cobblestones make excellent edging for paths; their tight-fitting shape makes them great for keeping gravel within boundaries. And, of course, cobblestones are a natural, if somewhat expensive, choice for driveways.

Veneer Stone

Veneer stone is specially cut into uniformly thick, flat-back pieces to make it easy to apply to the surface of a concrete-block wall. Standard veneer is 4 to 6 inches thick, while thin natural veneer is only ¾ to 1¾ inches thick; both are usually rectangular in shape. Standard veneer also works as a low path edging or stacked to make a short raised bed.

LEFT A concrete-block retaining wall was vastly improved by the addition of veneer stone. The same stone set into a concrete bed was used for the adjacent walkway.

OPPOSITE PAGE A path made of reused cobblestones adds an antique feel to this small garden. Almost as soon as stones are laid, they look like they've been there for hundreds of years.

Loose Materials

The term "gravel" refers to small stones that are either collected from natural deposits or manufactured by crushing larger pieces of stone. Crushed rock with its irregular edges packs together to form a more solid surface, making it easier to walk on. Naturally occurring gravel is made up of small rounded pebbles, which tend to roll around a bit when stepped on. This type is more often used as a decorative element or

between stepping-stones. Gravel comes in a variety of sizes and colors and makes a relatively inexpensive path material that provides excellent drainage. Both crushed and rounded types also work well as mulches for planting beds.

Decomposed granite, or "DG," is a popular material for casual paths and driveways. It is made up of tiny pieces of granite, from ¼ inch in diameter to sand size, in shades of

LEFT Gravel makes an ideal flooring for this casual patio. Entering the area, you hear a satisfying crunch underfoot as soon as you step off the last flagstone. Gravel also provides excellent drainage for the pots.

TOP RIGHT This classically proportioned walkway is made of decomposed granite between wide edging blocks. The slight color variations in the material only add to its charm.

RIGHT An inviting gravel path curves between a lawn and planting bed. An unobtrusive edging keeps the grass out of the path, and vice versa, but the perennials opposite are free to spill onto the path.

gray, tan, or reddish brown. To form a solid path, the material is laid onto an edged bed of crushed-stone gravel, then moistened and compacted. DG tends to erode with time, but various stabilizers and resins can be mixed in to make the surface more stable. One thing to keep in mind: DG, especially when wet, tends to stick to the soles of shoes. When tracked inside, it can act like sandpaper on wood floors.

Boulders

A boulder by definition is a detached and rounded or much-worn mass of rock. It may be huge or relatively small, rough-edged or smooth, but it is truly the most raw of materials, highly evocative of the natural landscape.

FIELDSTONE, perhaps the most familiar type of boulder, is any stone found lying in a field or buried beneath the soil. Fieldstones offered for sale in stone yards may also have been salvaged from an old wall or building that has been torn down. These rocks have been aged by being exposed to the elements and are often decorated with lichens or moss. Some are attractive enough to hold their own as garden sculptures (due to their varied colors and interesting shapes) and all are excellent for creating a primitive or antique look in the garden. Some are flat enough to use as rough stepping-stones or flooring for a rustic patio. If the shape is right, they can make interesting steps when set into a hillside.

QUARRIED BOULDERS have been blasted or dug from larger formations, so they often have angular, jagged surfaces that can be quite dramatic as focal points in a landscape. They may also have attractive veining of contrasting color. Basalt columns are tall, relatively narrow pieces of stone that can serve as garden accents or as fountains when a hole is drilled through them from top to bottom.

RIVER-WASHED BOULDERS have been smoothed and shaped by flowing water. These stones often have a more uniform texture than fieldstones, and their overall shape can be exquisitely graceful. Their rounded contours can be reminiscent of a Henry Moore sculpture, but, of course, at considerably lower cost. They are also a natural choice for water features.

WALL STONE, as its name indicates, is used to build dry-stack or mortared walls, though it can also be used for edging. Wall stone comes in two general categories: rubble, which is uncut or roughly squared, and ashlar, which is neatly trimmed into a block shape and can be laid almost as easily as brick.

OPPOSITE PAGE A simple planting scheme keeps the focus on these sculptural boulders. Partially burying the stones makes them look as if they are part of the natural terrain rather than recent additions.

TOP Rough-hewn quarried boulders hold back a hillside with muscular assurance. A slight dip in the wall's contour invites low-growing plants to tumble over its edge.

ABOVE This carefully planned composition features two river-washed boulders that echo the color and shape of the urns nearby. Soft-looking plants and smaller round stones fill out the bed.

Stone Medley

THIS PAGE This backyard packs a lot of appeal into a small space. The smooth flagstones and circular patio are in harmony with the house, while the faux stone–veneered wall and dramatic waterfall create an attractive contrast.

OPPOSITE PAGE, TOP What looks like a massive natural rock formation is actually a carefully designed recirculating water feature built into a steep hillside.

OPPOSITE PAGE, BOTTOM A narrow path of Connecticut bluestone leads around the house, past the waterfall, and into the backyard.

Landscape architect Karen Aitken designed this unique backyard stonescape in Gilroy, California; the complex installation was done by Mitsugu Mori of Green Valley Landscape in Salinas, California. The space artfully ties together a variety of stonework, including a covered circular patio connected to the house. Graceful wrap-around steps lead to the lower level, where an impressive water feature takes center stage without overpowering the space. Aitken's original plan called for just a small waterfall, but the owners were so taken with the idea, they asked

The Elements

- **Patio Floor.** Idaho quartzite flagstone is laid in a tight-fitted pattern, making a smooth, even surface for foot traffic and for patio furniture. A light-colored mortar was used between stones, and the entire patio was laid on a concrete base for stability.

- **Patio Steps.** The circular steps have risers made from the same Idaho quartzite as the floors, but the treads are of bullnosed Arizona flagstone.

- **Waterfall.** Massive rough-hewn boulders appear to have piled up naturally, forming the setting for a spectacular recirculating waterfall. Moisture-loving plants thrive at the foot of the falls.

- **Flat Boulders.** On either side of the waterfall, large boulders with broad flat faces are grouped and set into the wall for sculptural effect.

- **Side-Yard Pathway.** A winding pathway is fashioned from Connecticut bluestone set close together in soil, but still with enough space between for low-growing plants to soften the seams.

- **Retaining Wall.** Although it looks like natural stone, the wall is made of concrete blocks faced with manufactured El Dorado Stone veneer.

her to expand it to occupy a 24-foot section of the retaining wall. The sound of the waterfall buffers noise from the street, and it can be enjoyed from both floors of the house.

Manmade Materials

The word "stonescaping" usually refers to landscaping with natural stone, but manmade materials are sometimes the more practical or economical choice. Some materials are designed to emulate natural things, such as a concrete patio carved and stained to resemble genuine stone. Others, such as colorfully patterned ceramic tiles, are obviously fashioned to reflect an artist's hand. Still others possess an Old World charm, like that of antique bricks used to create a stylish patio, or concrete pavers laid in patterns reminiscent of those seen in ancient streets. And, of course, your choices are not limited to all-natural or all-manmade materials when it comes to your landscape: Some of the most interesting designs use elements of both.

Recycled or salvaged materials can also be used as stylish and relatively inexpensive landscape elements, either as structural components, like a raised bed made from pieces of a demolished concrete driveway, or as decorative accents, like a sculpture fashioned from twisted rebar.

ABOVE
A contemporary front-yard makeover features large stepping-stones made from concrete slabs. The concrete steps leading to the sleek wooden deck add to the modern, straightforward appeal.

TOP RIGHT Cleverly fashioned to look like stone, these steps and boulders are actually made of concrete poured and shaped in place. Pigments were troweled on during the drying stage to create the various hues.

RIGHT Winding through a colorful flower garden, this path of seeded-aggregate concrete and brick spacers is smooth enough to accommodate almost any kind of traffic.

Concrete with Added Color or Texture

When you think of concrete, visions of a cracked, oil-stained driveway may come to mind. But this inherently malleable material has come a long way in recent years. Poured concrete can be tinted during the mixing stage in a wide range of reliable, stable hues, and existing concrete can be given a facelift with chemical stains that produce rich colors in an attractively mottled pattern. Paints specially formulated for use on concrete give a more solid color,

much like that of painted wooden decks.

Smooth sidewalks are great for skateboarding, but if you'd like a more interesting texture for a concrete patio or path, you have options. Concrete is made from a mixture of portland cement, water, and aggregate (sand and gravel). The finished slab appears smooth because of a thin layer of cement that forms on the surface. This top layer can be removed just before the concrete is fully set to expose the aggregate, for a rougher,

LEFT A curving concrete entry walk is spiffed up by a border in a lighter shade of gray.

ABOVE Pigment, sawn lines, and texture applied to small squares give this patio its custom look.

more natural look and a less slippery surface. The same effect can be accomplished by sandblasting an existing slab to remove the top layer. Freshly poured concrete can be attractively roughened by various methods, such as brooming (creates fine lines on the surface), salt-finishing (results in randomly spaced pits of various sizes), or application of a travertine finish (looks similar to rough stucco).

For even more texture, you can carve or stamp designs into the surface of wet concrete. These impressions may be made in a grid pattern, for instance, to obtain a surface resembling cut stones placed close together, or in a more free form to give the effect of close-set flagstones. Stamped impressions of leaves, burlap, or even thin pieces of wood can add whimsy to stepping-stones or patio floors.

Additions to Concrete

Embedding small stones or pebbles in drying cement results in a finish known as seeded aggregate. This has long been a popular option because it gives the impression of a pebbled path—but the pebbles never move. Pieces of glass or tile can also be added to brighten a dull concrete slab, as can salvaged objects like seashells or scrap metal—basically anything that can be set flush into the surface before it dries.

You can also update concrete by completely covering it with another material, such as tile, stone, or brick. Do this only if the concrete slab is structurally sound or can be repaired as the first part of the makeover.

OPPOSITE PAGE
Smooth, flat river rocks set into concrete make an interesting surface for this side-yard garden path.

LEFT A mix of pebbles and remnant tile pieces was laid on a plain concrete pathway to create this whimsical leaf pattern.

Reusing Concrete

If your old concrete driveway or patio is beyond repair—or if you've just decided to replace it with another surface—you can make good use of the broken pieces that remain after the sledgehammer has done its work. The broken edge of concrete has an attractive pattern of embedded rocks of various sizes and colors. Since the chunks will be of a consistent thickness, they will work nicely as building blocks for a stacked wall or raised bed. These pieces also make interesting stepping-stones and stair steps.

RIGHT Thick pieces of broken concrete make an ideal material for a short retaining wall and stairs. The irregular shapes leave gaps that are just right for tucking in herbs and other plants that prefer good drainage.

Bricks

Brick has been made in basically the same way for thousands of years—by firing a mixture of clay and other materials in a kiln. Laid brick provides a handsome surface that blends well with almost any architectural style. It's a versatile, time-tested material that can be used to floor a patio, form or edge a path, or build garden walls and beds. Brick is quite sturdy, and it lasts a long time.

Bricks are available in a wide variety of earthy colors, from nearly black through a range of brown, red, and tan shades to gray and white. Metals may be added to the clay to produce dark speckling, and special firing techniques can give an interesting variety of effects, such as a darker face or edge to each brick. Brand-new brick in a solid color confers a contemporary, refined look, while used brick—or brick manufactured with a more rustic finish—brings an instant established look to the garden. This type of finish includes irregularities formed by heat in the kiln or white staining called efflorescence. Landscape designer Cameron Scott says, "I love using old, recycled brick, which really fits well with the character of some older houses."

Textures vary too, but there are two general types used for landscaping: Common brick has a rough, porous texture, while face brick has a more polished surface that is a bit too slippery for use on paths but makes a refined-looking raised bed or

edging. When it comes to shape, most bricks are roughly rectangular on their face, shaped like elongated cubes, though some types have rounded edges. Paver bricks are about half as thick as standard bricks and are made to be set atop a concrete base. "Cored" bricks have holes that are useful for holding extra mortar when building a wall. Here's a tip from garden designer Tara Dillard: "If you're using bricks with holes, never let the holes show."

OPPOSITE PAGE, LEFT A small brick patio like this one is easy to construct in a weekend, and just about any yard has space for its modest dimensions.

OPPOSITE PAGE, RIGHT Red paver bricks are a nice complement to the surrounding stonework.

ABOVE LEFT Fashioned from the same brick used on the house, this tailored patio is an extension of the main structure. Larger stone pavers are used for the adjacent path.

ABOVE A path of tawny bricks shows slight variations in color and texture, only adding to its charm. The bricks were laid on a bed of crushed gravel covered by landscape fabric and a top layer of sand. Concealed beneath the plants on either side are mortared brick borders that prevent shifting.

A concrete "stone" path curves through blue star creeper and Japanese spurge.

Concrete Pavers

Concrete pavers have come a long way from the days when they were offered only in uniform gray and pinkish tones and had a decidedly industrial look. Dealers now offer a variety of more natural-looking colors and varied shapes resembling brick, cut stone, or cobblestones. According to Tara Dillard, "Tumbled and stained concrete pavers can add an element of age, warmth, and personality, similar to that of stone."

Interlocking pavers are designed to fit together like pieces of a jigsaw puzzle, but simple rectangular or square pavers are also very stable when closely set. You can buy pavers in sets made to create circular or fan shapes or complicated repeated patterns.

Today's pavers are made from an extremely dense formula of concrete that is pressure-formed in machines. They are very durable, lasting well in most climates. And since pavers are relatively inexpensive, they're becoming more and more popular.

Stackable Retaining Blocks

Concrete stackable retaining blocks are designed to interlock, forming a wall solid enough to keep a hillside or garden bed in place. These too have come a long way from the early versions, and some achieve a look similar to that of real stone. More obviously manmade styles give a modern, industrial look.

Faux stone

Manufactured veneers made from lightweight aggregates are available in panel form for use on walls; high-quality types closely approximate the look of stone and brick. Recent innovations include a decking system comprising thin panels of natural stone laminated onto composite materials. You can also find fairly convincing fake boulders made from polyurethane or cast stone.

TOP The different sizes, shapes, and colors of these concrete pavers make for an interesting textural path.

MIDDLE This patio made from inter-locking concrete pavers in two sizes resembles a European courtyard.

BOTTOM The blocks in this wall are rounded on the front face, giving them a stone-like appearance.

Terra-cotta-colored
Saltillo tiles top a base
layer of cement to
form a casual walkway.

Ceramic Tile

Ceramic tile has a refined look that works well both indoors and outdoors. It's a great choice for a patio near the house, where you want to make just that transition. You can even use the same or similar-looking tiles in both areas.

Glazed tiles are the shiny types that often sport bright colors and detailed designs. They can be quite slippery, especially when wet, so unglazed tiles are a better choice for flooring. Since tile is relatively thin and fragile, it is normally laid on a concrete slab for flooring.

In cold climates, choose tiles that are not affected by freeze-thaw cycles. In mild climates, terra-cotta tile is fine for outdoor use. It often has quite a bit of color variation from tile to tile, making it a good choice for a casual look.

Use glazed tile to add splashes of color to landscape features, such as a fountain or birdbath. You can incorporate a few tiles here and there to enliven a flagstone path. Tile mosaics are particularly nice for tabletops.

ABOVE LEFT A patchwork mosaic of glazed tiles would be a visual jumble if used for an entire patio, but it's a great way to enliven small areas like these steps to the back door.

ABOVE RIGHT The smooth, shiny surface of glazed tile is perfect for use in water features like this patio fountain. Small, blue tiles give the interior the look of deep water, and the cheerful colors of the exterior can be repeated in surrounding plantings.

Recycled Glass

Here's an eco-friendly twist that you might consider as a colorful replacement for gravel or pebbles: recycled glass that's been tumbled to smooth the sharp edges. Available in a wide variety of colors, this material is probably best used in small amounts, perhaps as a top dressing for container plantings or as a mulch for limited "specialty areas" in the garden. Soft blue oceanic tones are particularly attractive.

Colorful glass mulch surrounds a shiny gazing globe.

Concrete Cool

THIS PAGE With its outside surface softened by grasses and New Zealand flax and its inner curve defined against the gravel patio, this dramatic wall delineates the landscape both spatially and texturally.

OPPOSITE PAGE, TOP Ever-changing shadows and light play out on the smooth concrete wall, while the gently overflowing fountain adds glitter and splash.

OPPOSITE PAGE, BOTTOM A linear stucco wall seen from poolside creates a right angle with a slatted fence. Concrete coping, aqua tiles, and a fountain fashioned from a bronze pipe make this area a work of functional art.

Landscape designer Bernard Trainor designed this renowned garden in Los Altos, California, just south of the San Francisco Bay. Centered in the view from the living room windows, a recirculating fountain fashioned from a shallow bowl forms a subtly shimmering focal point. Curving around it is a concrete wall that is the perfect height for seating; it also separates the space near the house from the wilder landscape beyond without obscuring the view. The wall stretches between two pairs of Chinese elms originally planted decades ago by the

celebrated landscape architect Thomas Church. A second, linear wall serves as a boundary between the entry and the pool area beyond.

The Elements

- **Curving Wall.** The S-shaped concrete wall was poured in place in two sections. After the forms were removed, the surface was hand troweled to give it a smooth, organic surface with natural variations in color.

- **Bowl Fountain.** A wide low-profile concrete bowl constantly overflows into a bed of gravel. The bowl rests on a grate that conceals a water reservoir containing a recirculating pump.

- **Gravel Walk.** For the wide walkway near the house, Trainor chose Hollister round rock, a ¾-inch gravel that is large enough not to be picked up in shoe treads and tracked into the house.

- **Linear Wall.** With a plaster surface that perfectly matches that of the house, a straight wall makes a striking contrast to its curved counterpart. At night, unobtrusive uplights turn the taller wall into a glowing highlight.

- **Pool with Fountain.** A rectangular swimming pool surrounded by rugged plants fits this landscape's aesthetic perfectly. To bring the sound of running water to the garden, a bronze pipe extends from a poolside hedge of dwarf olives and spills water into the pool in a never-ending stream.

Mixing It Up

One of the great things about designing outdoors is that you can feel free to mix materials as you like. Just because you have a flagstone path doesn't mean that you have to use the same material for raised beds or walls. According to landscape designer Bernard Trainor, "Mixing manmade and natural elements can be very sharp, expressing grounded and manipulated aesthetics simultaneously." And garden designer Tara Dillard says it's perfectly fine to mix and match, even within the realm of one element: "If you're on a tight budget, use old bricks from several sources to create a landscape with character."

OPPOSITE PAGE A casual flagstone path leads to a round patio of textured, stained concrete bounded by a stone wall with brick coping. Each material makes sense where it's being used, and all work well together visually.

TOP LEFT This small patio was made from recycled materials, including aluminum letters of various sizes and chunks of reclaimed black slate.

TOP RIGHT Perhaps the person installing this patio ran out of flagstones and had to use materials at hand, including bricks, an old piece of tile, and a few flat pebbles. Or maybe she just liked the way they all looked together.

MIDDLE LEFT These concrete tiles were stained to match the hues of the river rocks set between them.

MIDDLE RIGHT Shiny, dark pebbles are set into the mortar of this flagstone patio for an organic-looking accent.

BOTTOM The contrast of these rough boulders with the smooth, regular surface of the concrete steps accentuates the character of both materials.

ABOVE Though the stone elements—cut stone, veneer, and boulders—differ in texture and form, they all work together nicely in this patio with a wall fountain.

LEFT The pebbles in this impressive oriental-carpet effect complement the hues of clay pots, wooden garden furniture, and the dark slabs of the raised bed.

RIGHT Simple and effective, a casual flagstone path cuts through an expanse of crushed gravel of a similar hue.

Natural Stone at a glance

Natural Boulders

- **Pros:** Good for decorative use and walls. Flat fieldstones can be used for paving; river-washed boulders for ornament and in water features.
- **Cons:** Irregular shape can make them difficult to use for some projects. River-washed boulders are too smooth for paving.
- **Price:** $–$$
- **Installation:** For use in paving, set flat side up in bed of gravel or sand. As decorative elements, can be set directly in soil.
- **Green Tip:** Choose local stone to eliminate long-distance transport.

Quarried Boulders

- **Pros:** Rugged and strong looking, with angular shape useful for building walls, raised beds, benches, and rock gardens.
- **Price:** $–$$

- **Installation:** As decorative elements, can be set directly in soil. Wall stone, whether rubble (rough blocks) or ashlar (fairly uniform blocks), is ideal for dry-stacked or mortared walls.
- **Green Tip:** Choose stone from a local quarry to cut down on transport.

Flagstones

- **Pros:** Irregular shape gives a natural look to paving and walls. Wide range of colors and sizes.
- **Cons:** Can be difficult to fit together; may require cutting.
- **Price:** $–$$
- **Installation:** Thick flagstones can be set in soil or sand. Thinner ones should be set in mortar on a concrete base.
- **Green Tip:** Leave an unmortared gap between paving stones for increased permeability and to reduce runoff into local storm drains and water supplies.

Cut Stone

- **Pros:** Formal appearance makes it a good choice for paving and for facing walls. Square or rectangular shape makes it easy to piece together.
- **Price:** $$–$$$
- **Installation:** Thick stones can be set in soil or sand. Set thinner ones in mortar on a concrete base.
- **Green Tip:** Choose stone from a local quarry, to cut down on transport. Leave an unmortared gap between paving stones to increase permeability and decrease runoff.

Cut stone

Natural boulders

Cobblestones

- **Pros:** Uniform shape and small size make for easy paving or edging. Very durable. Add a look of Old World charm.
- **Cons:** Create a somewhat uneven surface. Require an edging to stay in place.
- **Price:** $$–$$$
- **Installation:** For paths, set on a bed of sand. For driveways, set on a tamped bed of gravel topped by sand. As edging, simply set in soil.
- **Green Tip:** Use recycled cobblestones.

Veneer Stone

- **Pros:** Gives a concrete wall the look of a stone wall. Uniform, lightweight pieces relatively easy to work with. Comes in many colors and textures.
- **Price:** $$–$$$
- **Installation:** Set in mortar on concrete-block wall, or stack for low raised bed.
- **Green Tip:** Requires less stone quarried than for full-thickness stone.

Veneer stone

Crushed Gravel

- **Pros:** Compacts firmly to make a solid base good for paths or as a foundation layer under pavement. Available in many sizes and colors.
- **Cons:** Can lodge in shoe treads and scratch indoor floors. Requires edging to stay in place on path.
- **Price:** $–$$
- **Installation:** For a path, install edging first, then a layer of sand, then gravel at least 2 inches thick.
- **Green Tip:** Gravel paths are highly permeable, allowing water and rain to seep into soil rather than run off into storm drains and water supplies. Crushed gravel available as reusable waste from quarries.

Rounded Gravel

- **Pros:** Highly decorative. Available in many colors and sizes, including fairly large decorative pebbles.
- **Cons:** Shifts and rolls, making it harder to walk on than crushed gravel. Requires edging to stay in place on a path.
- **Price:** $–$$
- **Installation:** Same as for crushed gravel.
- **Green Tip:** Lets rainwater seep into ground rather than run off into storm drains.

Cobblestones

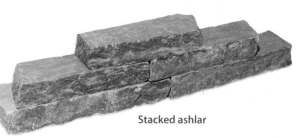

Flagstone sampler

Stacked ashlar

Gravel sampler

ABOVE This elegant entryway plays up the contrast between brick and stone. The refined-looking brick was chosen for its varied tones of red, and the ashlar blocks in the walls for similarity to colors of the house.

LEFT A study in contrasts, large rust-colored pavers are each framed with small, square pavers in darker shades.

RIGHT These concrete pavers were poured in place, then dressed up with smooth black-pebble inlays.

Manmade Materials at a glance

Poured Concrete

- **Pros:** Durable and easy to maintain. Can be stamped, colored, or decorated with inlays.
- **Cons:** If not textured, can be slippery when wet.
- **Price:** $$–$$$
- **Installation:** Best left to an experienced professional.
- **Green Tip:** Ask your contractor about permeable paving that allows rainwater to soak into soil. If adding color, use nontoxic pigments.

Brick

- **Pros:** Available in a variety of colors, textures, and shapes.
- **Cons:** Moss can grow on bricks, making them slippery. Brick walls can be tricky for a do-it-yourselfer to build.
- **Price:** $–$$
- **Installation:** For paths, lay brick on sand or mortar over a concrete base. Choose SX-rated bricks if you live where the ground freezes and thaws. Brick walls require mortar; consider hiring a contractor or brick mason.
- **Green Tip:** Use salvaged bricks. Faux "used bricks" may actually be concrete pavers.

Concrete Pavers

- **Pros:** Widely available in many shapes and colors. Easy to maintain.
- **Cons:** Can have an industrial look.
- **Price:** $–$$
- **Installation:** Requires a permanent edging to prevent shifting. Pavers are installed over compacted gravel topped with bedding sand. Interlocking types stay in place without mortar.
- **Green Tip:** Permeable pavers reduce runoff into storm drains.

Stackable Retaining Blocks

- **Pros:** Ease of installation; durability.
- **Cons:** Lower-quality types can look industrial.
- **Price:** $–$$
- **Installation:** Stacked or pin-locked systems can be set on a concrete base or gravel bed.
- **Green Tip:** Use fibrous or aerated concrete blocks.

Faux Stone

- **Pros:** Lightweight veneer panels are easy to install; can look like the real thing.
- **Cons:** Inexpensive types can look fake.
- **Price:** $$–$$$
- **Installation:** Panels are attached to walls with mortar or adhesive.
- **Green Tip:** Can give the look of exotic stone without transporting the real thing over long distances.

Brick sampler

Ceramic Tile

- **Pros:** Vast array of colors, sizes, and shapes. Gives an elegant, finished look to paving and walls.
- **Cons:** Glazed types can be slippery when wet.
- **Price:** $$–$$$
- **Installation:** For paving, choose strong, weather-resistant tiles, whether glazed or terra-cotta. Set them in a bed of mortar on top of a concrete slab. Many types require a preservative seal.
- **Green Tip:** Choose tiles made of recycled materials.

Recycled glass

- **Pros:** Available in many colors. Can be striking in the landscape as mulch, attractive in containers. Choose ⅜-inch or finer grade tumbled glass.
- **Cons:** Large areas can be overwhelming, with a distinctly artificial look.
- **Price:** $$–$$$
- **Installation:** Easy to spread from bags. Use landscape fabric underneath to keep soil out.
- **Green Tip:** Keeps glass out of landfills.

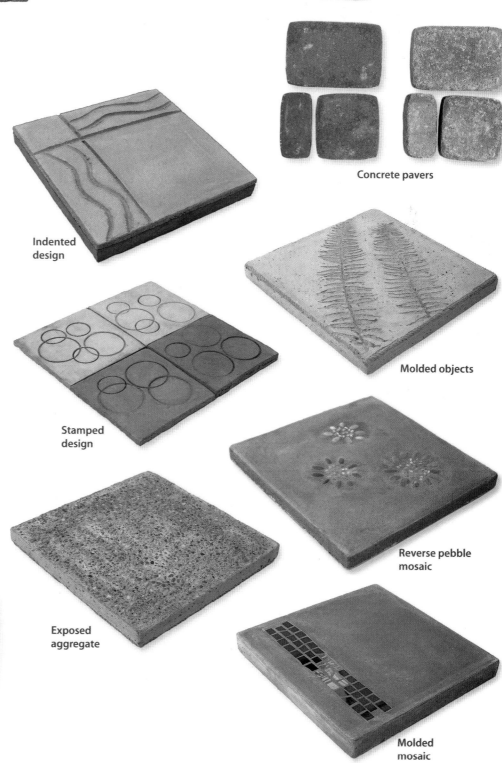

Concrete pavers

Indented design

Molded objects

Stamped design

Reverse pebble mosaic

Exposed aggregate

Molded mosaic

Ceramic tile sampler

Chapter 2

Patios

Whether it's just outside the kitchen or at the far edge of your property, a patio invites you out of the house and into the realm of sunshine, fresh air, and growing plants. Once you've created a convenient, comfortable spot outdoors, you'll find yourself returning to it often, taking a little journey without leaving home. You may choose to keep it simple, with a cozy bench and a few flowerpots, or you may want something more elaborate, like an outdoor kitchen or a formal space surrounding a splashing fountain. In this chapter, you'll find plenty of ideas for creating the perfect patio for your home.

Design Considerations

You may already have some ideas about which materials you'd like to use for your patio, but consider these two important and related questions before you proceed further: How will the patio be used, and where should it be located?

Function First

When designing a new patio or planning a make-over for an existing one, take time to think about how you'd like to use your outdoor space. Do you just want a place for a couple of comfortable chairs when you take a break from gardening, or a secluded spot where you can sit on a bench to catch the warmth of the morning sun? Do you want a place for family dining and cooking? Maybe you'd like to entertain outdoors, with casual seating around a fire pit or a more formal dining area. What about places for kids to play or for pets to claim as their special domain? Consider all the ways you might want to use the space, then move forward with your design accordingly.

ABOVE A patio featuring an appealing collection of pots and sophisticated furniture is nestled into a corner alcove.

LEFT This small patio is simply a wide place in the curving path, strategically placed to afford a spectacular view and to take advantage of the trees' shelter.

RIGHT Too narrow for a table and chairs, this passageway affords a perfect place for an angled bench beneath an arbor. A sphere-shaped fountain welcomes you into the space.

Location, Location, Location

If you're planning a new patio, take care in choosing where to place it in relation to your home. Take a walk around your property (whatever its size) and imagine how you might create outdoor spaces suited to different activities you have in mind.

Patios look best and get the most use when they are partially enclosed, perhaps located next to the house or bounded by a hedge, fence, or even just a collection of shrubs in large pots. But don't completely surround your outdoor space—you'll want to leave at least one side open to a view, be it a distant hilltop, the neighbor's stately oak tree, or a water feature at the opposite end of your main garden path.

Choose a bright spot for your patio over one with constant deep shade. Don't forget to take the weather and seasons into account. If you live in an area with hot summers, you might situate your patio where it will be in the dappled shade of trees during the hottest part of the day. Or plan for an overhead structure like a vine-covered arbor, a retractable awning, or even a simple umbrella.

GARDEN DESIGNER
TARA DILLARD ON

Patio Placement

If you are planning on having just one patio, place it off the kitchen and be generous with its size. A patio stretching from your kitchen to family room or a guest room can change how you use your home and raise your property's value."

feature. A third type of patio space is what I think of as a room with a view—perhaps a couple of Adirondack chairs at the edge of a lawn overlooking a vista or even simply looking back at the house."

Keep or Replace?

If your property includes a concrete patio that is too small, outdated, or unattractive for your taste, consider your options before rushing to remove it. You might be able to lay flagstones or pavers on top of the patio; if it adjoins the house, however, you'll need to be sure the elevation change is not too great at the threshold. To make an existing patio larger, you can also add pavers or flagstones around the edges as an accent. According to landscape designer Bernard Trainor, "Provided the patio is in good structural condition and is in scale with the house, the greenest, most sustainable thing you can do is to keep it, perhaps changing the color by staining or altering the texture by sandblasting. If your patio is situated in the wrong spot or the material is not to your taste, however, it's best to take it out."

One or Several?

Houses are frequently built with a single patio in the backyard, often adjacent to the kitchen or den. This is what some landscape designers call a primary patio. It should be designed to transition smoothly to the indoor space, perhaps by using flooring materials or furniture style and color that are similar indoors and out.

But why stop at just one? Most properties can accommodate another smaller patio or two. According to landscape architect Karen Aitken, "A secondary patio is often a private space, around a corner, screened by plants, or off a master bedroom. This is meant to be more of a quiet, contemplative space, and it's often a good spot for a water

A few general principles of design are worth mentioning here. These are not hard-and-fast rules, but they can help you achieve a cohesive, considered look for your patio.

UNITY All the elements of your patio should blend together through a common theme or harmonizing color scheme, especially near the house. This doesn't mean that you can't have variety and some elements of surprise. You can take risks outdoors that might seem over the top indoors.

PROPORTION Make sure your patio is in scale with the house and garden. When in doubt, go larger: The great outdoors calls for size. If a single large patio is in order, break up the space into smaller areas—perhaps a group of chairs in one area and a water feature in another. In a small patio design, keep things simple and consider gardening vertically using hanging pots or trellises. Don't hesitate to include a large, dramatic element in a small space.

BALANCE Don't create a space that feels uneven, with a large feature on one side of the patio and nothing on the other. A patio tree might be visually balanced by a pair of chaise longues beneath an umbrella.

FOCAL POINTS A patio, like any room, benefits from a point of interest, such as a flowering tree, an eye-catching statue, or even a distant view. Garden lighting can bring out a special feature that is particularly stunning at night, even when seen from indoors.

OPPOSITE PAGE All elements of this rustic patio demonstrate unity of design. The boulders around the stream are similar in color to the flagstones, and the fire pit incorporates both types of stone. The rough-hewn furniture is a great choice; imagine how out of place formal wrought-iron chairs would look.

ABOVE LEFT For proper proportion, this large area called for a good-sized patio beneath a big, dramatic arbor. A wide path and generous steps are perfectly in scale, as are the oversize flower bowls.

TOP RIGHT Water features make great focal points, especially those that can be heard as well as seen. This contemporary fountain invites you to take a stroll around the corner patio.

BOTTOM RIGHT This small, freestanding pool might look stark and out of place if not for the balancing effect of the curved planting bed next to it.

The most inviting patios usually include some sort of furniture. This might be a simple stone bench where you sit for a moment while admiring nearby plants, or a well-padded chair where you can settle down with a good book. Side tables and coffee tables are widely used on patios, serving the same utilitarian functions they do indoors. If you plan to have meals outdoors, of course you'll want a table and comfortable chairs.

When choosing furniture for your patio, there are a few things to keep in mind, such as how the legs will rest on the floor. The thin legs of iron chairs can slip between flagstones, for instance, making the chairs hard to keep stable and level. For landscape designer Scott Colombo, the scale of outdoor furniture is critical: "Oversize teak furniture looks fine on a 30-by-30-foot terrace, but it can easily overwhelm a smaller, intimate space. I encourage clients not to buy too much

LEFT This expansive patio has room for a dining table and chairs, chaise longues, and side chairs. The arrangement of the furniture, as well as the large pots, can be reconfigured for different types of gatherings.

TOP RIGHT Even though it's only a few feet from the dining table, this stone bench evokes a feeling of privacy.

RIGHT A wrought-iron bench along the path invites you to pause on the way to the table. From that vantage point, you'll take more notice of the filigreed gazebo adorned with hanging lanterns.

furniture. I have seen many patios so overstuffed they look like a furniture showroom! Also, I advise people not to plan patio size or furniture quantity on that one big party they might have every year or so."

Be sure there's enough room for circulation around patio furniture. This is especially important for dining sets: Allow 3 to 4 feet around the perimeter of a table to give diners room to push out their chairs and to walk around the seated table.

Seating Areas

LEFT Here's a great little conversation area featuring cool open-mesh chairs gathered around a focal point of patterned stone tile.

RIGHT This casual seating area includes a table and chairs where adults can relax, and a set of wide steps (made of reused concrete) that serve as bleachers for the kids.

When thinking about how to arrange a seating area, take a cue from your indoor rooms. A bench (usually about the size of a small sofa or love seat) flanked by a couple of chairs makes a comfortable and good-sized conversation area. Or place a couple of chairs off by themselves with a table between them for a more intimate setting. Especially as you get farther away from the house, feel free to mix styles and materials. Not every seating area has to be created from a matched set.

When it comes to placement of patio furniture, landscape architect Craig Bergmann suggests that you avoid putting the primary seating area within the main view from the home. "You don't want to have to look through an outdoor room of furniture in order to see the landscape beyond," Bergmann says. "If there are spatial constraints and this can't be avoided, try to integrate sculptural pieces and planted containers in the immediate foreground to distract the eye."

STONE CONSULTANT JAN NIELSEN ON

Stone Seating

Garden furniture takes a real beating from the weather for much of the year in the Pacific Northwest, so I like to use stone benches and low walls for seating. Wide stairs also make excellent seating areas, like bleachers or an amphitheater. The stair steps should be at least 5 to 6 feet wide so people can sit, turn, and have a few feet between them for socially comfortable distance."

Comfort is key in outdoor seating areas. Provide soft lighting and thick cushions, especially when the area is protected from weather with an overhead structure.

OPPOSITE PAGE
Keep a few lightweight folding chairs handy, and you can create your own seating areas on an as-needed basis. This spot just off the front porch is sun-drenched during the morning hours but cool and shaded in the afternoon.

TOP RIGHT In this plant lover's backyard, the chairs are oriented toward the dramatic stone terraces that step down to the patio. The landscape seems to be spilling toward you when you're seated here.

RIGHT A wide pathway at the bottom of these stairs is an ideal spot for a light and graceful set of antique furniture. Sunken gardens help to create privacy because surrounding plantings gain extra height from the grade change.

TOP LEFT Tucked beneath a winding staircase, this intimate table makes a fine place for enjoying hors d'oeuvres or a light supper. Easily accessible from the house and lighted by glowing lanterns, the dining area is as appealing as any outdoor cafe.

BOTTOM LEFT Set back from the house but connected to it visually by a wide flagstone walkway, a slightly raised patio accommodates a dining table large enough for full-scale dinner parties. The fence, umbrella, and rose standards all contribute to a comfortable sense of enclosure.

RIGHT A black metal furniture set is just the thing for this small dining area right outside the house. A bold black planter showcases a New Zealand flax as a structural element, and a water feature tempts you to take a seat on the bench at the patio's far end.

Dining Areas

Why is it that food somehow tastes better when you dine outdoors? Maybe it has to do with the novelty of the setting—outside the usual kitchen or dining room—or perhaps it conjures memories of good times around a family picnic table. Do the fresh air and connection with nature heighten your senses in some way? Whatever the reason, the popularity of outdoor dining is undeniable. It's one of the main reasons people add patios to their homes.

Outdoor seating areas where you sit only briefly can be less than luxurious, but when you're settling in for a meal, you want to be comfortable. Make sure the patio surface is level

and the furniture stable. If possible, locate your dining area beneath the shade of a tree or add a vine-covered arbor, pergola, or umbrella to your patio design. Overhead protection is not essential in mild areas unless you're planning to dine alfresco year-round, but it does give a sense of enclosure and comfort. Where summer evenings are cool, consider a fire pit or outdoor heater.

Lighting can make all the difference in an outdoor dining room that will be used at night. Make sure there are no dark spots between the house and the table if your guests will be carrying plates or glasses, especially where steps are involved. Rather than harsh, bright floodlights, choose the soft glow of candles in glass hurricanes, lanterns hanging from hooks along the path and set about the patio, or perhaps a string of tiny white holiday lights strung on a tree or arbor overhead. Landscape designer Scott Colombo may include an outdoor chandelier if the site is right, as well as an all-white planting scheme that seems to glow after dusk, fragrant plants that may be beyond the eye's reach, and a subtle water element to add soothing burbling sounds.

LEFT A patio extending from the house is an ideal spot for this wooden table and chairs. In the comfortable evenings of summer, this is a favorite destination when it's time for dessert or after-dinner drinks.

BOTTOM This dining area sits on a raised patio surrounded by lush, multihued plantings. Though only a short distance from the house, it has the feeling of a remote and magical place.

OPPOSITE PAGE Even a tiny backyard has room for an area set aside for dining. At the end of a flagstone path, a single step up beneath a post-and-beam portal lets guests know that they've arrived.

LANDSCAPE DESIGNER BERNARD TRAINOR ON

Dining Areas

It's particularly nice to have a dining area that is somewhat removed from the house. Why have a dining room directly off the dining room? A water feature or specimen plant in a soft spotlight will help to draw you outside. If possible, situate your outside dining area near edible plants, like beneath a fruit tree or next to an herb garden. Tomatoes seem to taste better when eaten in view of the vines from which they came."

Outdoor Kitchens

When it comes to outdoor kitchens, there are two general strategies you can take: simple or elaborate. A simple setup might include a portable grill and a small table for food preparation. Charcoal grills of the old-fashioned kettle type are still popular and some people swear by the taste of foods cooked in charcoal smoke. Portable gas grills are most commonly fueled by propane tanks, which have to be changed periodically, but you can also opt for a connection to your home's natural gas line. The latest generation of portable gas grills offers plenty of fancy features, such as rotisseries, tool holders, spotlights, and multiple burners that allow you to cook different foods at the same time. Some even have built-in smoker boxes so you can get that desirable wood-smoke flavor.

A more elaborate outdoor kitchen can include most of the conveniences of one inside the home, including cabinets, expansive counters, built-in grill and burners, sink and faucet, refrigerator, and perhaps even a pizza oven. Before you embark on a full-scale outdoor kitchen, consider carefully how often you will be using it; once you start adding features, the project can quickly get quite expensive. And whatever you include, don't make the cooking area too large unless you plan to use it

LEFT This linear kitchen includes everything you need to prepare and cook meals alfresco. A dual-level counter makes serving convenient, and guests can enjoy watching their meal being prepared, or give grilling advice ("Better flip those burgers now").

TOP RIGHT A low stone wall with a built-in grill snuggles up to shrubs and potted plants at the lawn's edge. Consider growing culinary herbs like rosemary, sage, and thyme near your outdoor kitchen for the freshest possible seasonings.

BOTTOM LEFT Just a few steps from the house, this stainless-steel grill fits nicely into an attractive stone niche, with well-placed task lighting overhead. The wooden bench doubles as a storage unit for cooking utensils and other supplies.

BOTTOM RIGHT A simple portable grill can be tucked into the corner of almost any patio and rolled out when needed.

regularly for entertaining large groups. Another option is to use a portable grill for everyday grilling and a larger outdoor kitchen for weekends and entertaining.

A few practical notes: Locate your outdoor kitchen near the outside dining area and not too far from the kitchen door. Make sure to place your cooking unit away from anything flammable, like wooden fences. Take into account the smoke your barbecue will produce and the direction of prevailing winds. If countertops are part of your design, you might heed the advice of landscape architect Karen Aitken and use simple concrete. "This is the easiest surface to clean and is quite forgiving when it comes to stains," Aitken says. "Also, concrete doesn't show dust like granite and tile do." And a final note from landscape architect Craig Bergmann on the unpleasant reality of rodents: "Even grease-covered grill brushes can attract them. We recommend stainless-steel box cabinets set into masonry surrounds, with wood attached to the outside face of the doors for a warmer look. It's also important that masonry surfaces surrounding the grill—not just the countertop—are scrubbable."

Comprehensive Kitchen

THIS PAGE Ideal for entertaining, this spacious patio has plenty of room for a fully equipped kitchen and a dining area. Small cafe tables can be moved around as needed.

OPPOSITE PAGE, TOP Plaster walls are painted in a warm golden hue that picks up similar shades in the stonework and terra-cotta pots.

OPPOSITE PAGE, BOTTOM A ceiling of hand-hewn wooden beams helps create the feeling of an actual room. A bonus: It takes more than a rain shower to spoil a dinner party here.

I n the mild climate of Healdsburg, California, it's comfortable to dine outdoors during most of the year, so the owners of this lovely Tuscan-style home decided to go all out on their new alfresco kitchen and dining patio. The 16-by-22 foot space sits beneath a roof of wood beams and terra-cotta tiles supported by stout stone pillars. For maximum convenience, the kitchen includes most of the amenities of its indoor counterpart, plus a gas-fired barbecue and a handsome raised fireplace that bathes the space in flickering firelight. There's plenty of

The Elements

- **Paving.** Buff-colored Arizona flagstone was mortared onto a concrete base for a smooth, finished floor.

- **Stone Columns.** As attractive as they are functional, the hefty support posts were constructed from Osage limestone.

- **Fireplace.** Elevated to the level of the counter-tops, the easily accessible hearth of the fire-place sits atop a cubby designed for storing firewood. A full-featured, gas-fired barbecue with side burner becomes the focal point at mealtime.

- **Cabinets.** Tawny concrete counters top the smooth-troweled plaster walls of the cabinets. Rugged wooden doors feature wrought-iron hardware.

- **Sink.** Fully plumbed with hot and cold running water, a large soapstone sink sits to one side of the fireplace.

- **Pantry.** Built into the wall adjoining the house is a pantry that contains a full-size refrigerator, trash containers, and shelves and drawers for kitchenware.

- **Lighting.** Hanging iron lanterns provide soft ambient lighting, while unobtrusive spotlights are positioned to illuminate task areas.

room for a large dining table, and the adjoining stairs and landing are perfect for informal seating nearby.

Poolside Areas

Swimming pools are typically surrounded by a paved area where kids can play and adults can relax. For pools located away from the house, this area may be widened into what is essentially a poolside patio. Pools closer to the house are typically joined to it by a patio, which serves as a transition from indoors to out. People are attracted to water, and even if they aren't going to take a swim, guests are likely to walk out onto the patio to have a look at the pool.

Naturally, poolside areas should be paved with a nonslip surface. Seeded-aggregate concrete is a traditional choice, but cut-stone pavers and natural flagstone can serve beautifully too. The coping, where the patio meets the pool's edge, must be smooth enough for contact with skin and bathing suits. Landscape designer Scott Colombo says, "Although many pools have a contrasting coping band, I prefer a seamless blend of pool coping to the surrounding patio." Some pools incorporate boulders at the water's edge, a look that works particularly well with naturalistic pools but can also be striking in contemporary designs. Take into account the hardscaping beyond the patio as well: Don't use loose materials like gravel

LEFT This multilevel patio is perfectly designed to link the house to the pool. A low stone wall doubles as a bench, and a small waterfall provides a gentle splash that lures the homeowners outdoors.

TOP RIGHT Poolside plants need a rugged constitution to thrive. This combination, which includes a tree mallow, two types of rosemary, white 'Flower Carpet' roses, and an olive topiary, fits the bill.

RIGHT A screened-in porch connects the house to a bluestone patio surrounding an inviting blue-tiled pool and spa. Ornamental grasses soften the hardscape and draw your attention to the breeze with their gentle sway.

or patio bark on paths leading directly to the pool, as they'll inevitably end up in the water.

You'll need to take safety considerations into account for your poolside area. Check into local laws regarding protective barriers; often a surrounding fence or wall at least 4 feet high is required at some point between your pool and areas of public access. Safety covers for swimming pools and spas must be able to bear considerable weight and have no gaps through which a small child could crawl.

Poolside Furniture

Gone are the days of the aluminum-frame chaise longue strung with sticky plastic tubing. The poolside furnishings available today are nearly as stylish and comfortable as indoor pieces. Choose sturdy, durable furniture, since it will get a lot of abuse from sun and water. A few chairs and a small table or two make for a pleasant grouping near a pool. And everyone loves to stretch out on a chaise longue; place two with a low table between them or line up several in a row to give everyone a place to relax. Patio umbrellas may be freestanding or designed to fit into a table. Either way, they're a welcome relief from the sun, and they offer an easy way to add a big splash of color to your poolside design.

These substantial chaise longues are in complete harmony with the stone patio and the wooden furniture in the garden beyond. Thick, comfortable cushions are covered in durable material of white, which won't discolor in the sun.

ABOVE Where summers are particularly hot, pools benefit from the dappled shade of surrounding trees. A bright umbrella in a table base echoes the pool's hues and offers further protection from the sun.

RIGHT Simply elegant, these contemporary chaise longues look just right with the grid-style patio surface. Grasses and other small-leafed plants keep the edges from looking too harsh.

Fireplaces and Fire Pits

W hether gathering with friends or family to roast marshmallows or gazing into the flames in solitary meditation, people enjoy being near the glow of fire. There are several ways to bring fire into your space.

Fireplaces

An outdoor fireplace makes a patio feel like a cozy room. It can be built at the edge of a patio, next to the rear wall of the house, or anywhere on the property that can accommodate a fairly large hardscape feature including a chimney of some height. Incorporate a fireplace into an entertainment area

along with an outdoor kitchen and plan for comfortable seating in front of the hearth. Be sure to include a convenient covered spot for storing firewood.

Building a masonry fireplace can be expensive, so you might consider a prefabricated unit instead. Gas-burning types are available and produce less air pollution than wood-burning models. Some gas models are front-vented; the exhaust is released through slots in the face frame, so a chimney is not needed. Zero-clearance units can be framed and finished with stucco, stone, or tile. Other prefab fireplaces are stand-alone art pieces that don't need to be finished on-site.

OPPOSITE PAGE
Even when it's too warm for a fire, the glow of large candles in an elaborate candleholder attracts visitors to a stone fireplace with built-in seating area.

TOP Centered in a circular gravel patio, this handsome fire pit is made to match a semicircular stone bench. This is a spot where people are guaranteed to gather.

BOTTOM LEFT This kettle-style fire pit comes with a screened lid to prevent firebrands from escaping into the wind.

BOTTOM RIGHT A chimenea fitted with a spark arrester and screen complements the fitted flagstone terrace.

Fire Pits

Fire pits are a favorite choice among those who design gardens. Landscape designer Bernard Trainor is an enthusiastic proponent: "If you live where the evenings get chilly even in summer, your money is well spent on one of these." Pits can be designed to burn wood, propane supplied by a tank, or natural gas from a permanent line off the house. "Gas models are particularly nice," Trainor says. "The fire emerges from rocks, glass, or ceramic material that resembles real logs. Colored glass works beautifully; it's a lively focal point in the light of day, and at night, you notice the flames, not the glass." Built-in stone fire pits are another popular option and are often designed to include a bench where you can sit and enjoy the warmth and flickering glow.

Portable Fire Features

Almost any patio can accommodate a small, portable fire pit, easily moved with the changing seasons or for parties. For a little more enclosure of the flames, consider a chimenea (Spanish for "chimney"), a diminutive freestanding fireplace with an open front for loading wood and a chimney for venting smoke.

Where There's Smoke

When choosing a site for your wood-burning fireplace or fire pit, be sure to take into account the prevailing winds, lest smoke blow into the house or directly toward the seating area. Many areas of the country have restrictions on wood fires because of concerns about air pollution and wildfires. Be sure to check local ordinances. Consider wood substitutes, such as logs made from wax or recycled materials, including a sweet-smelling type composed mainly of coffee grounds and molasses.

Fire Safety

A few commonsense precautions should be mentioned. Never leave a fire unattended. Choose a spot for your fire feature that is well away from combustible plants like dry grasses and evergreens. Make sure your fire pit is stable and level, and set it up on a hardscape patio of stone, concrete, or gravel; patio bark is flammable. Chimneys should be fitted with spark arresters, and fireplace screens help reduce the hazards of escaping embers.

TOP ROW In perfect scale with the stone patio and low wall, this simple red fire pit makes a stunning focal point.

A rustic fireplace featuring local river stones and a wide slab hearth hugs a corner of the house.

As stylish as an interior room, this contemporary patio features a stucco fireplace painted lemon yellow.

BOTTOM ROW This low-slung stone fireplace in soft shades of tan and white offers plenty of warmth and light without blocking the view beyond the fence.

After a long day of surfing, this is the perfect spot for chilling out by a warm fire.

LANDSCAPE DESIGNER
SCOTT COLOMBO ON

Patio Heaters

If your garden plan doesn't include a fireplace or fire pit, consider incorporating patio heaters. These extend the season for outdoor living in any part of the country, and newer styles are more attractive and less industrial looking than old ones. Most are tall freestanding units, some are designed to replace an umbrella in the center of an outdoor dining table, and others are tabletop models that are easy to move around the patio."

Garden Getaways

Patios are often thought of as places for entertaining, but sometimes you just want to get away from it all, to retreat to a little spot in the garden where the tranquility of nature rules. Landscape designer Bernard Trainor reflects on patio design: "For decades, the trend has been to locate patios right off the house, like outdoor rooms, with the garden elements farther away and somewhat remote. We're moving back now to drawing people directly into the landscape. All you need is a sort of 'green veil' between your home and your garden getaway, where you can surround yourself with plants and hardscape materials that nourish your hunger for nature."

Gardens of just about any size have room for a private retreat. You might create a secret path that leads through an opening in the hedge to a tiny patio just large enough for a bench. A back corner of your yard is a likely location, but even close to the house you can create a secluded spot. Side yards are prime candidates because they often afford privacy. If your property includes an elevated area, you can make a little hilltop perch. Even a corner of an existing patio can be partially enclosed by a bamboo screen and a couple of potted shrubs.

Regardless of the spot you choose for your getaway, you'll want to make sure it's comfortable. An outdoor daybed with overstuffed cushions is a

ABOVE Tucked away in a woodland corner, this cozy getaway—just a bench at the end of a pathway—makes a perfect spot to rest and reflect.

LEFT Two comfy chairs facing a panoramic view and a patio umbrella create a pleasing respite from the busy world.

RIGHT From this lofty site, you get a different perspective on the garden and, perhaps, on your day.

great place for reading or taking a nap, and you can create something similar with a plain wooden bench and a couple of outdoor pillows. Perhaps you have some out-of-date garden furniture or a mismatched piece or two that you've picked up at a rummage sale. Even indoor furniture that has seen better days can work perfectly well outdoors in summer, though you'll want to protect upholstered pieces from rain. A couple of Adirondack chairs and an old stump to prop up your feet make a good place for an intimate conversation. In your own little outdoor space, there are no rules except your own.

When it comes to plants, surround your getaway with your personal favorites without worry about the principles of design. This is a good place to experiment. Fragrant plants are particularly nice for a sanctuary garden, as are those with edible parts, intricate flower forms, and soft fuzzy leaves. All encourage you to use your various senses to get back in touch with the green world around you.

GARDEN DESIGNER
TARA DILLARD ON

Creating a Summerhouse

Even in a tiny yard—and on a tiny budget—you can build a lovely little summerhouse. Start with a rectangular stone floor large enough for a pair of chairs. Install sturdy posts in concrete at the corners, and add a sloping shingled roof. Attach a back wall, leaving three sides open, and—if you can—run electricity to the structure, perhaps for a ceiling fan."

Special Touches

To make your garden getaway even more appealing, include features with a particular quality that speaks to you. This could be something as simple as a wind chime or a gazing ball. Place your chair so that you have a view of a bird feeder across the garden. Install a small statue or even a simple standing stone, with low, spreading plants at its base. Water features are particularly good at helping you to attain the quietude you seek in a getaway. Even a small birdbath or a modest recirculating fountain helps set your mind at ease.

TOP LEFT A glazed yellow pot draws your attention to the small patio, where a comfortable-looking deck chair creates a pleasant temptation.

BOTTOM LEFT This whimsical variation on the "hot tub" theme includes screening plants and an ancient bathtub plumbed for hot and cold water and set on a stone slab.

TOP RIGHT Wooden chairs in a setting of greenery are placed inside a circular patio edge designed to suggest peaceful enclosure.

BOTTOM RIGHT A painted metal chair set on a simple stone patio invites you into a small hideaway resembling a clearing in the woods.

You could easily while away an afternoon in this secluded getaway complete with a wooden bench, a splashing fountain, and a hammock in the shade.

Patio Plants

We've looked at surfaces and furnishings for outdoor rooms, but without the presence of foliage and flowers, these could be stark and uninviting places. A patio needs plants, and they can be included in three basic ways. Around the perimeter and extending overhead, trees, shrubs, and vines give the patio a sense of comforting enclosure. In the intermediate layer, somewhat smaller plants fill in, whether spilling onto the patio at ground level or presenting visual interest at eye level. And of course, container plants bring greenery onto the patio itself.

ABOVE A carefree mix of herbs and perennials hugs this sunny patio. A potted tree and a verdant shrub mark the patio entry.

TOP RIGHT To accommodate the tropical plants they love, the homeowners built this elegant atrium, complete with a retractable skylight and a pond for koi.

BOTTOM RIGHT A contemporary black planter box makes a striking visual screen between house and patio.

Patio Trees

The ideal patio tree is relatively small, with a well-behaved root system that won't crack or lift pavement. Choose a disease-resistant tree with special features that appeal to you, such as flowers, fruit, good fall color, or interesting bark. Most trees drop some litter in the form of flowers, fruit, or seedpods—and deciduous trees lose their leaves completely in fall or winter—but this may require only minimal cleanup once or twice a year. Large evergreen conifers like pines and cedars tend to drop litter almost year-round. Deciduous trees are a nice way to take note of the changing seasons, and they shade the patio in summer but let in more light in the winter months.

Among the many great deciduous patio trees are small maples, serviceberry, redbud, dogwood, smoke tree (*Cotinus*), crape myrtle, small magnolias, flowering crabapple, sourwood, and flowering cherry. For year-round cover, choose an evergreen tree such as citrus, small types of cypress (*Cupressus*), michelia, fruitless forms of olive (*Olea*), smaller palms, fern pine (*Podocarpus*), or evergreen pear.

Green Screens

To add privacy to your patio or to block wind or noise, plant a hedge of evergreen shrubs that are leafy and full from top to bottom. Examples include boxwood, bottlebrush, hop bush (*Dodonaea*), evergreen types of holly, juniper, privet, photinia, smaller types of pittosporum, arborvitae, and evergreen types of viburnum. Clumping bamboos make great hedges too.

To mix things up a bit in your hedge, include a few deciduous shrubs that make up for their wintertime leafless-ness with colorful flowers or interesting foliage. Try hedge maple (*Acer campestre*), European hornbeam (*Carpinus betulus*), flowering quince, beauty bush, winter honeysuckle (*Lonicera fragrantissima*), shrub roses, or weigela.

Climbing Color

If you have a plain fence or unattractive wall alongside your patio, why not decorate it with a lush-looking flowering vine? Or add an arbor or trellis to your design and dress it up with greenery. The choices among vines are too numerous to list here, but be sure to pay attention to the way your preferred vine climbs. Some will cling to almost any surface by way of holdfasts or aerial rootlets (these may cause damage to some building materials). Other vines climb by twining stems or tendrils, so they need something relatively small in diameter to coil around, such as a trellis or chain-link fence. Still others, such as climbing roses, are not really vines at all but scramblers with no means of attachment; these must be tied to a support.

CLOCKWISE FROM NEAR RIGHT Though exposed to the open sky, this large patio feels protected by the large trees at its perimeter. Smaller trees and shrubs are placed closer in, and large pots of sweet potato vine guide you through the space.

Flaming with fall color, this Japanese maple is just the right size for its spot alongside a stone patio.

A casual little patio snuggles up to a stately stand of bamboo. When the breeze blows, the whole area is filled with a soft rustle.

In a small space, go vertical. Hanging baskets and jasmine trained into a diamond pattern against the wall thrive in the dappled shade of a wispy patio tree.

Loaded with fruit, a grape vine trained onto a small arbor makes a green roof for this gravel patio. In fall, the leaves color nicely, and in winter, the leafless vines let in more light.

Fillers and Edgers

When choosing plants of low and medium height to include around your patio, you are limited only by the garden conditions, such as soil type and sun exposure. Choices include everything from small flowering shrubs to evergreen ground covers and perennials; from ferns and bulbs to herbs, grasses, and annuals. You can arrange these into a mixed border, with lots of colors and textures, or you may wish to go with a more uniform look, using large sweeps of a single plant.

Since you'll be experiencing them up close, choose flowers with intricate details or a sweet perfume for your patio. Plants such as herbs and scented geraniums have wonderfully fragrant leaves, especially when brushed against, and fine-leaved grasses have a soft texture perfect for hiding the harsh edge of your patio's paving. Roses are an obvious choice, but place them (as well as any other plants with prickles or thorns) back a bit from the patio's edge. Another thing to keep in mind: Plants situated immediately adjacent to a sunny patio need to be able to handle the reflected heat of the pavement.

HORTICULTURIST
BALDASSARE MINEO ON

Low-Growing Edging Plants

For shady areas, I recommend bergenia, carpet bugle, coral bells, and hosta. Some favorite plants for sunnier spots are thrift, rockcress, basket-of-gold, ice plant (*Delosperma*), many of the smaller phloxes, and candytuft."

LEFT When seated on this circular stone patio, you feel enclosed by the grasses, New Zealand flax, and tall sages. When standing, you can see into the garden beyond.

RIGHT A heat-loving verbena spills attractively onto a gravel patio.

MIDDLE Foliage softens the edges of this casual patio of decomposed granite. Monolithic boulders enclose the space.

BOTTOM Small flowers and ground covers from this eclectic edging border have invaded the flagstone patio, with charming results.

Container Gardening

Filling containers with interesting plants is a surefire way to add color and texture to your patio. Most plants grow well in standard potting soil available from garden centers, but a few, like rhododendrons and cactus, do better in specialty mixtures. Remember that plants in containers are completely dependent on you for their nutrition, so feed your potted plants according to package recommendations. Some gardeners prefer to water their containers by hand, but most like the convenience of drip or spray systems on automatic timers. If possible, plan your system so that the tubing doesn't show; for instance, by installing PVC pipes beneath a flagstone patio, with T-connectors emerging near your planned container area.

Plants for Containers

Some designers like to stuff pots with as many different plants as possible, creating a "living arrangement" of contrasting colors and textures. Others prefer the "one pot, one plant" look, with a single plant—or several identical plants—filling the container. It's really a matter of taste. Or you can use a mixed scheme: several plants in a container for a seasonally rotated display, and a single specimen for more permanent container planting.

Do keep in mind the mature size of the plant and its rate of growth. Roots need room to spread, but if the container is too large, the extra soil can become sour and develop diseases. Landscape

LEFT Succulents planted in an assortment of containers thrive in the heat reflected from a stucco wall.

TOP RIGHT Against a background of aquatic grasslike perennials and leafy border plants, sculptural bowls planted with cactus and succulents are a study in contrast. A stone trough makes an ideal home for herbs.

BOTTOM LEFT A yellow dish simply planted with baby's tears sits securely on a bed of smooth river stones.

BOTTOM RIGHT Chalky white containers in an elegantly mismatched trio hold tropical plants with boldly contrasting leaf shapes and colors.

architect Craig Bergmann uses these guidelines: "If the container is 16 inches or less in diameter, I typically use a single one-gallon pot to fill it. If the container diameter is greater than 16 inches, I plant it with two or three one-gallon pots—possibly underplanted with smaller accents or trailers. When the container is very large, 36 inches or more, I plan for six or eight one-gallon pots, or three or more larger pots of foliage plants."

Many trees are well suited to growing in large containers, among them small pines and palms, yew pines (*Podocarpus*), Japanese and fullmoon maples (*Acer palmatum* and *A. japonicum*), and dwarf trees like 'Little Gem' magnolia. Many citrus and dwarf forms of apple and fig also make fine container subjects.

Most shrubs will do quite well in pots; choose those that stay relatively small or at least grow slowly. Roses grow well as long as they have a sufficiently large container, and smaller bamboos thrive in pots, where even the most aggressive running types are not a worry.

When it comes to flowering perennials, annuals, grasses, succulents, ferns, vines, and bulbs for patio containers, just about anything goes. Do make sure that combination pots contain plants with the same basic needs in terms of sun, water, and drainage. Edibles are an excellent alternative (or addition) to flower pots. Tomatoes, rosemary, sage, chives, basil, and strawberries are just a few of the many choices.

Choosing Containers

Patio containers may be terra-cotta pots, glazed urns, wooden planter boxes, plastic hanging baskets, or just about anything you fancy that will hold soil and allow water to drain freely. Unglazed terra-cotta is porous, so the soil within dries out more quickly; glazed clay pots keep soil moist longer. Both are fairly heavy, which helps with stability but hinders portability. Terra-cotta is also somewhat fragile and is easily chipped or broken. Wood is a durable, weatherproof choice for a container. Better-quality plastic containers can be a good lightweight alternative, especially since they've come a long way in terms of style. Unless you have a gravel patio, you may want to purchase underliners to keep water from staining the patio surface.

When choosing a container, especially a large or prominently placed one, remember that it will have at least as much visual impact as the plants it holds. In the words of garden designer Tara Dillard, "Never buy a container unless it is so fabulous it could be empty and still be a focal point in your landscape." Scott Colombo, landscape designer, adds, "Often, I choose the container first for its beauty and ability to enhance the patio or landscape. I typically keep them simple; I especially like to use antique pots and urns that are beautiful on their own. Sometimes, I don't even plant them out. This allows for plants to be placed in them for special occasions or during a specific season."

Designing with Containers

When it comes to the scale of patio containers, a common mistake is to purchase ones that are too small. Landscape designer Bernard Trainor has some advice: "When you're shopping for a patio container, pick one in a style you like, then double the size! A too-small pot can look pitiful against the large scale of a house or patio. Also, the smaller the pot, the more often it will need watering."

In a formal patio design, identical pots may be placed symmetrically around the space; for a more casual look, choose a variety of containers. Choose ones with a common thread that ties them together—for instance, five pots of a similar color but of different shapes and sizes.

OPPOSITE PAGE, LEFT A white cube filled with a broad-leafed shrub makes a bold statement against a contemporary fence.

OPPOSITE PAGE, RIGHT Pots of different shapes and sizes, in a similar warm color, hold a lively mixture of plants in burgundy, white, and green.

ABOVE LEFT Set off by a lemon-yellow wall, this concrete pot of gun-metal gray is a perfect match for the leaves of a bronzy phormium.

ABOVE RIGHT This stuffed ceramic bowl can be easily moved around the patio, and as individual plants outgrow it, they can be moved into the garden.

Plant-Packed Patio

THIS PAGE This spacious patio has plenty of room for several comfortable seating areas in the shade of a vine-draped arbor.

OPPOSITE PAGE, TOP The luxuriant fragrant blooms of 'Rose de Rescht' are held aloft next to aromatic thyme creeping over the stone wall's cap.

OPPOSITE PAGE, MIDDLE In the foreground, purple heliotrope thrives in a container of mixed plants. Against the house, 'New Dawn' rose and 'Henryi' clematis mingle in a classic partnership on the trellis.

OPPOSITE PAGE, BOTTOM A stylish metal orb rises from the "reverse parterre," with boxwoods creating solid geometric shapes within the space rather than outlining them as they would in a traditional parterre.

L andscape architect Craig Bergmann created this lovely garden for a converted coach house in Lake Forest, Illinois, on Chicago's North Shore. All of the garden's elements were designed to match the Arts and Crafts style of the home. A sunken rose garden is surrounded on three sides by inviting patios, lushly planted beds, and a clever twist on a parterre garden theme. The main patio features a built-in fountain and comfortable seating in the shade of a wisteria-draped arbor. On warm summer evenings, the intoxicating fragrance of roses lingers in the sunken space, much to the owners' delight.

The Elements

- **Patio Floor.** The main patio of New York bluestone overlays a concrete slab that originally served as the foundation of a greenhouse.

- **Steps.** The wide steps connecting the upper and lower levels are made from rough-edged slabs of buff-colored Wisconsin Lannon stone.

- **Walls.** The mortared walls of Lannon stone surrounding the sunken garden make a beautiful backdrop for roses, lady's mantle (*Alchemilla mollis*), and catmint. Some sections of the wall were left with open tops, where fragrant thyme thrives.

- **Gravel Path.** Tying together the two levels is a gravel path made from crushed bluestone—the same material used in cut-stone form for the patio floor.

- **Fountain.** A freestanding fountain reminiscent of a small fireplace is made from Chicago common brick capped with limestone. The splashing sounds echo softly through the courtyard and bring the space to life.

- **Containers.** Rectangular terra-cotta planters at the top of the stairs hold seasonal plant compositions; shown here are fragrant purple heliotrope and chartreuse licorice plant (*Helichrysum petiolare* 'Limelight').

- **Reverse Parterre.** Bergmann inserted a whimsical note by trimming boxwoods, traditionally used to edge small geometric areas, into solid shapes surrounded by 12-inch-wide slabs of bluestone.

Chapter 3

Paths and Steps

A firm, stable surface underfoot lets you move comfortably around a garden, freeing you to focus your attention on the pleasures of leaf and bloom rather than on how to make your way through the space. Walkways fashioned from stone and stone-like materials also provide a sense of structure, giving visitors instant clues about how the space is organized. In this chapter, explore a variety of ways to add beautiful, durable paths and steps to your landscape, from simple gravel walks to elaborate stone stairways. All are invitations to stroll through the garden.

Design Considerations

Here, the stepped pathway is the focal point of the landscape. Like water flowing down the hill, it tempts you to follow its course and discover what lies around the bend.

P aths and steps are functional necessities that keep your feet off the soil and out of the mud and allow you to navigate slopes easily, but they are also design elements. For most garden situations, stone and stone-like materials are an excellent choice. The materials contrast beautifully with greenery and, if correctly laid, create walkways that are practically permanent.

A main path or stairway is one that connects the house to a primary destination, such as a pool, a vegetable garden, or the street. Place main walkways with traffic flow in mind, creating direct routes, and choose a paving surface that is fairly smooth. Make these paths and stairs at least 3 feet wide, or a minimum of 5 feet wide to allow two to walk side by side comfortably. Choose a style and material that make sense with the look of the house. An elegant, traditional home might call for cut-stone steps and a matching path, whereas a more rustic house might look best with granite slabs for steps and a fieldstone walkway.

Farther away from the house are secondary paths and steps, which become more prominent design elements on their own. They afford an opportunity to switch to different, and perhaps more informal, materials and styles.

LANDSCAPE ARCHITECT
CRAIG BERGMANN ON

Path Destinations

"P aths should always lead to a destination, but this might simply be a spectacular meadow or an uncrossable brook at the edge of your property. Your feet may stop, but your eyes continue. A path that leads through plantings and stops abruptly at the edge of a lawn is unsatisfying, but by adding a few stepping-stones in the lawn, you can suggest transition and continuation."

In general, a path should lead to something, not just dwindle away or come to a dead end at a fence or hedge—though of course there can be stopping places along the way. One way to slow down the journey is to place a curve in the path, but try to make it curve around something rather than veer randomly here and there. And make sure your path curves broadly and gracefully, not in a tight "squiggly" way.

Gardens on steep hillsides require steps or stairs for access. But even on a gently sloping site, consider adding a step or two to mix things up a bit, perhaps introducing a different type of stone or using the opportunity to change planting schemes.

TOP LEFT A casual secondary path of flagstones leads from a backyard patio, past a flowery trellis, toward a mysterious stone plinth.

TOP RIGHT Steep slopes call for regular, comfortably spaced steps and a handrail for added safety. The sharp curve at the bottom ensures that you'll pause for a look around the garden.

BOTTOM This gracious entry path begins with a couple of wide, inviting stone steps. A tall lantern and flanking boulders reinforce the impression of a main entry.

Paths

Generously sized flagstones with rounded edges are spaced to match the stride of the gardener.

Whether they're fashioned from close-set pieces of flagstone, gravel held in place between cobblestone edgers, or pebbles set in concrete, stone paths provide a sturdy walking surface for garden floors. Tailor your choice of path style and material to the uses you plan. If a path must accommodate the frequent use of a wheelchair or a tricycle, it should be flat and relatively seamless, such as one made of mortared flagstones, brick, or close-set cut stones. A path intended for slow strolls through the garden can be more open and casual, perhaps with room for fragrant ground-carpeting plants between stepping-stones.

A few practical considerations are worth mentioning. If possible, do not route your path next to trees with aggressive roots, and avoid perpetually wet areas of the garden. In all cases, good drainage is important. Most of the paths described here include some sort of base material such as gravel to help drain moisture away from the path. A good rule of thumb is to build your path slightly pitched to one side; runoff needs only about ¼ inch of slope per foot. Paths made from loose materials should be slightly higher in the center so that water won't pool there.

Stepping-stone Paths

A stepping-stone path is one of the easiest to design, because it basically matches the steps of a person's natural gait. Just like footprints in the sand, a stepping-stone path can be made to zigzag slightly, with one step a little to the right of center and the next a little to the left. Designers suggest placing the stones at a fairly constant distance from one another, and orienting them so that the longest dimension runs across the path, not in the direction people walk. Stepping-stones can be set flush with the soil level (convenient if you plan to run a lawn mower over them) or just slightly above it.

Garden centers and stone yards offer a wide variety of choices for stepping-stones, from rough fieldstone to smooth Arizona flagstone and molded concrete pavers in squares and circles. In the case of natural stone, choose pieces with a relatively flat top and bottom for ease of installation, and don't skimp on size: The best-suited stones are at least 18 inches wide, 15 inches long, and 2 inches thick (up to twice as thick if you want elevated stepping-stones). Pick out a few especially large, attractive pieces for the beginning and end of your path, or plan to set several pavers together at those points.

Stepping-stones can be laid directly on soil, but they'll be steadier if you excavate a shallow hole for each stone that is the same shape and about half as deep as the stone is thick. Then add a layer of sand at least 1 inch deep, and wiggle the stone into place.

GARDEN DESIGNER
TARA DILLARD ON

Stepping-stones

Stepping-stones create functional and aesthetically pleasing paths while being easy to install yourself, provided the terrain is fairly flat. Stones set about an inch apart create a beautiful visual ribbon from a distance and are easy to walk on without having to look down at where your feet are landing. Stepping-stone paths can look quite different depending on their surroundings. In a shady area, surround them with small wood chips or patio bark, and in sunny spots, spread pea gravel around them."

TOP Concrete pavers laid in an edged bed of stone chips make for a simple, contemporary path in perfect keeping with the home's architectural style.

ABOVE LEFT Set firmly into a gentle slope, these rough stones form a path that focuses your attention on each step, almost like scrambling up a rocky incline.

ABOVE RIGHT Rectangular stepping-stones of various dimensions march across a lawn. Mowing over this path is not a problem.

LEFT Flagstone set in mortar provides a surface almost as smooth as an interior floor, and it's just as easy to sweep clean.

BOTTOM LEFT Intersecting paths of round concrete stepping-stones and rectangular flagstones appear to be held together by living green mortar.

BOTTOM RIGHT An inspired stone garden features a substantial wall and a rocky water feature. The fieldstone steps seem to march right down to ground level to become a path.

OPPOSITE PAGE A path assembled from small local fieldstones winds through a shady garden carpeted with moss and decorated by ferns. Just about any other path material would look out of place in such a natural garden.

bit of space between the flagstones for tucking in low-growing plants. Another option is to set flagstones in wet mortar, which allows you to lay pieces as thin as 1 inch. With either method, an edging will help hold everything together.

Fieldstone Paths

Fieldstones have a more rustic look than flagstones, with rougher surfaces and more variation in shape and color, so you might want to use them a little farther away from the house. When shopping, look for stones with two relatively flat faces and, if possible, of equal thickness.

For a small fieldstone path, you can just excavate a shallow hole for each stone, add sand to the base, and drop each into place. For a path covering a larger area, you may want to excavate the entire path to a depth 2 inches deeper than the thickest stone, fill the area with gravel, and place the field-stones on top. Use sand in the joints. If a stone has a protruding area that prevents a good fit or makes a high spot, don a pair of goggles and chip away with a hammer and chisel.

Flagstone Paths

Paths made of close-set flagstones are popular for their natural elegance. They have the smooth surface of a more formal material like cut stone or brick, but their irregular edges have a pleasingly random quality. If you're planning on having plants and flowers flow over the edge of your flagstone path, use larger pieces toward the center and smaller stones at the edges. If the whole path will be visible, lay the largest stones along the edges and fill in with smaller pieces.

Flagstone can be laid on a bed of gravel topped by a layer of sand, in which case the stones should be at least 1½ inches thick. Fill the joints with sand. You can trim pieces for a very close fit or leave a

Cut-Stone Paths

Cut stone is popular for formal entry paths and main walkways because of its smooth surface and uniform appearance, but it can also lend a more playful feeling. Big slabs of stone cut into squares or rectangles can be arranged in a regular grid, using pieces of the same color, or in a more casual arrangement using different shapes and hues. This type of stone always has sawn edges and a flat back, but the top surface may be left natural or finished in one of several textures. To ensure good traction, choose a texture that's not perfectly smooth.

A path made of heavy cut stone, such as slabs of bluestone 2 inches thick and 2 feet square, can be laid in a simple bed of sand, with an added base layer of gravel for poorly drained sites. Paths made from smaller, lighter pieces need a firm edging to keep the stones from shifting. Cut stone's uniformity makes it a good choice for setting in mortar over a concrete path in need of a makeover. For this type of application, you can choose thin pieces, just 1 to 1½ inches thick.

LEFT Large segments of cut stone in various shapes and sizes make a generous path across a large garden.

RIGHT A cobblestone path calls to mind the streets of old and makes a pleasingly textured surface underfoot.

Cobblestone, Brick, and Concrete-Paver Paths

Paths fashioned from cobblestones, bricks, or concrete pavers have a fairly uniform look, being composed of small, thick pieces of consistent size; however, each of the materials can be used for very different effects. A cobblestone path instantly gives the feeling of antiquity to a garden. Used brick can give the same impression, especially when laid in a casual pattern, whereas new brick set in a formal pattern has a more finished look. Concrete pavers can be used to interesting effect, especially in a

contemporary garden design or where you can take advantage of prefabricated sets that form circles or other patterns when laid according to directions.

Cobblestones are usually installed on a base of gravel and sand, but they need an edging to stay in place and should be set closely together with sand-filled crevices. Bricks can be laid tightly against each other on a bed of gravel and sand, or they can be mortared onto a stable concrete slab. Most concrete pavers are designed to interlock, making for easy installation and a smooth path surface.

LEFT "Frogged" bricks, stamped with the name of the manufacturer, turn a used-brick walkway into a conversation piece.

RIGHT Pavers designed to resemble cobblestones give this garden path a rustic look combined with a smooth surface.

Gravel Paths

Gravel paths are a favorite of landscape designer Bernard Trainor. "I'm a gravel fanatic!" he says. "I love its texture, its high permeability and low cost, and most of all, the wonderful sound it makes when you walk on it. Gravel is a very experiential material."

Gravel paths are also quite easy to install, since you don't have to worry about fitting stones together, and there are enough colors and textures available to suit any taste. Rounded gravels tend to roll around a bit and will migrate off the path more quickly than crushed-stone material. Gravels that include fine particles make a sandy surface that is almost silent underfoot.

Edgings are usually required to keep gravel paths from dissipating into surrounding areas. Whether cut-stone, metal, plastic, wood, or brick, the edging itself can also function as a design element.

To build a gravel path, excavate the area to a depth of 6 to 8 inches and, if you wish, cover with a layer of landscape fabric. Then install the edgings along the sides. Add one or more layers of crushed gravel as a base material, wetting and tamping it firmly before adding your choice of path gravel.

Mixed-Material Paths

Pathways need not be made entirely of one material. You can use an assortment of ingredients to cook up your own look. Fill the spaces between square pavers with pebbles, different types of stone, or even glass bricks embedded with solar-powered lights. In a cut-stone path, add an occasional strip of stone turned on its edge and set flush with its neighbors. Pebble-mosaic paths are another way to get creative.

CLOCKWISE FROM NEAR RIGHT A well-tamped path of decomposed granite will maintain its integrity even without edging, especially on level ground.

Packed tightly together between painted-brick edgers and set into a base of cement and sand, the colorful pebbles of this artistic path will stay in place indefinitely.

Where different types of path materials meet, why not emphasize the transition? Here, smooth river stones accomplish that beautifully while also providing an area of excellent drainage.

Low brick "soldiers" make an informal edging for a gravel path flanked with hydrangeas.

This wide gravel path is a perfect fit for the Mediterranean style of the house and surrounding landscape. Plants like 'Hopley's Purple' oregano thrive in the reflected heat and excellent drainage that the gravel provides.

GARDEN DESIGNER
TARA DILLARD ON

Pathway Edgings

The edging pieces bordering a path are called 'soldiers,' since they march along in line and keep the path in order. The higher the soldiers, the more formal your path will look, and you can vary them with the type of path. For a gravel path, install stone or brick soldiers that rise at least 2 to 3 inches above ground level. This will keep the gravel in place, and it helps your pathway make a strong visual statement."

Pathside Plants

ABOVE Bright, fragrant nemesias make a long-blooming edging for this flagstone path. In cooler months, pansies and violets will be planted to continue the color show.

When it comes to deciding what to plant alongside a path, there are no hard-and-fast rules. Pathside plants will be subject to close inspection, however, so choose ones with close-up visual interest, great fragrance, or soft, touchable texture. You don't have to line your walkways with evergreens, but keep seasonal rhythms in mind: A path solidly lined with bulbs won't be so pretty when the foliage is fading. To unify a pathway and to keep the eye moving along it, repeat the same plant, such as a compact evergreen shrub, here and there on either side. And finally, keep in mind the mature size of your pathside plantings. It's nice to brush against plants, but you shouldn't have to struggle to get past them.

Gravel-Path Gardens

With drought becoming the norm in much of the country, interest in unthirsty plants is increasing. But many of these plants will not grow well where water fails to drain quickly away from their roots. Gravel provides excellent drainage when spread thickly on top of the soil as a mulch. This allows plants adapted to arid regions, for example, to thrive in parts of the country that receive regular rainfall. Gravel also reflects heat, which is a plus for many drought-tolerant plants in cooler climes. So consider widening your gravel path into a gravel garden populated by plants like Adam's needle (*Yucca filamentosa*), penstemon, coreopsis, heath (*Erica*), evening primrose, fountain grass, lavender, rockrose, and verbena, as well as succulents such as stonecrop and live-forever (*Sempervivum*). Culinary herbs like rosemary, oregano, and sage also thrive alongside gravel paths.

LEFT Upright sedums, fountain grasses, and bright yellow daylilies thrive in the well-drained conditions provided by a wide gravel path.

In-Path Plants

In order for plants to grow between stepping-stones or in the cracks between pavers, they have to be tough enough to survive the harsh growing conditions as well as some foot traffic. But that doesn't mean you can't have pretty flowers, like those of carpet bugle, English daisy, snow-in-summer, blue star creeper, *Mazus reptans,* and many violets, including *Viola labradorica*. Some plants release a pleasing fragrance when stepped upon, like chamomile (*Chamaemelum nobile),* Jewel mint of Corsica, and many low-growing thymes, including creeping thyme and woolly thyme. Others are stalwart plants whose main appeal is good-looking foliage for most of the year, like *Dichondra micrantha,* green carpet, dwarf mondo grass, Irish moss, baby's tears, and Korean grass. Check with your local nursery for the best in-path choices for your area.

LEFT Blue star creeper makes a durable long-blooming carpet between stepping-stones.

RIGHT Chamomile, sweet alyssum, and low-growing thymes pleasantly perfume and crowd this casual path.

BOTTOM LEFT A zigzag of dwarf mondo grass separates pavers in this lushly planted pathway.

BELOW This pathway composition includes unthirsty low-growing thymes and pale yellow yarrow between the stones, and lavender along the edges.

BOTTOM RIGHT Scotch moss and dwarf sweet flag (*Acorus gramineus* 'Pusillus') create an in-path composition of contrasting forms, colors, and textures.

Proper Paths

THIS PAGE At this main intersection, three paths come together: a path of wide-set concrete pavers in patio-style arrangement on the left; a linear path of close-set pavers leading directly to the raised patio; and a gravel path that leads in the other direction.

OPPOSITE PAGE, TOP Here the path widens into a casual patio comprising concrete pavers and fragrant thyme. Upright reed grasses (*Calamagrostis* x *acutiflora* 'Karl Foerster') grow at the house side of the patio in front of a wall of California wild grape *(Vitis californica)*.

OPPOSITE PAGE, BOTTOM As the pavers approach the gravel patio, they become even more widely set, leaving plenty of room for the spreading carpet of thyme. A single dramatic specimen of reed grass marks the spot.

The Elements

- **Pavers.** In keeping with the contemporary architecture and clean lines, Trainor had concrete pavers of various sizes poured in place.

- **In-Path Plants.** Surrounding the pavers are woolly thyme (*Thymus pseudolanuginosus*) and elfin thyme (a particularly compact form of *T. praecox arcticus*). Both are creeping plants that grow less than 2 inches tall and are soft and fragrant underfoot.

- **Pathside Plants.** In this drought-tolerant garden, stalwarts like yarrow, California poppy (*Eschscholzia californica*), santolina, and various sages hug the paths.

- **Gravel Path.** A local source provided the $3/8$-inch Metz gravel used for the path. Its light color harmonizes with the concrete pavers as well as the wall.

- **Cut-Stone Patio.** The plant-lined main path leads to the slightly raised patio; in this more formal area near the house, the paving changes to close-set, mortared paving stones set on a concrete base. A concrete ring creates a sculptural fire pit.

- **Gravel Patio.** In another area where the path widens, the same Metz gravel was used as flooring. This patio is planted with thyme and grasses, and bounded by a graceful wall of Montana wall stone.

I n this contemporary rural garden created by landscape designer Bernard Trainor for clients in Carmel Valley, California, a fitting array of tasteful path materials was used to connect the different outdoor living areas. Along one side of the remodeled ranch-style house, the path widens into a checkerboard patio interplanted with fragrant ground covers. Where the patio narrows to intersect the main path, the pavers line up more closely. Turning in one direction leads you around the house to a slightly raised patio featuring a fire pit. Taking the opposite path, your feet crunch along a gravel path to a small gravel patio bounded by a handsome stone wall.

Steps and Stairs

To quote landscape designer Bernard Trainor: "Steps are such a great design tool. When people change levels, they slow down and take in a new view as they reach the next elevation." There's a sense of repose when you reach the bottom of a set of stairs, and a feeling of accomplishment and discovery when you get to the top. You can build on that "garden moment" with a design that embraces it. You might place a bubbling fountain near the bottom of a stairway, for instance, or a sundial at the top.

Practically speaking, outdoor stairways should be in scale with the site, which usually means that they will be wider than interior stairs. In the garden, you want a feeling of leisurely ascent and descent, not that of a cramped space to be rushed through. Where a path meets the steps, make them at least as wide as the path. The steps themselves must be in proportion with people. Each step should have a riser (the vertical part of the step) between 4 and 7 inches tall. The tread (the horizontal surface where you actually step) should be

Outsized slabs of cut bluestone turn this hillside into a work of modern art in the landscape.

ABOVE Nestled between boulders, this gracious stairway includes several terraces that offer a chance to rest and take in a bug's-eye view of the plants spilling down the slope.

RIGHT Inset pebbles on the stone landing match the darkest tones in the surrounding wall, and the cut-stone steps match the lightest.

BELOW A picturesque stairway complete with rustic log banister invites you to begin a journey through the wooded hillside. Follow the yellow-leafed plants.

13 to 17 inches deep. Landscape architect Karen Aitken says: "I find that 7-inch-high risers and 14-inch-deep treads are perfect for most situations. And to avoid tripping problems, make sure all the treads are equal."

When the journey up or down the stairs takes more than five or six steps, you may want to include a landing to give people a chance to stop and rest. On very steep slopes, a zigzag design makes the climb easier. Consider adding lighting near steps, particularly when there are just a few steps that people might not be expecting.

Simple Steps

Casual-looking steps can be made to blend into the landscape, as if a few stones just happened to settle at a spot where the elevation changes. As landscape designer Scott Colombo notes, "Large chunks of stone artfully placed can make for simple, beautiful steps." Or steps can be used as design elements that boldly accent the horizontal lines that mark the changes in elevation.

Simple steps can be fashioned from overlapping stone slabs set into the hillside and leveled. Or you can use slabs at least 1½ inches thick for treads and make risers from smaller stones, bricks, or other materials. For more stability when small stones are used, set them in mortar. Another popular option is to build frame-style steps from rot-resistant timbers and fill them in with gravel.

LEFT Tucked between small sentinel boulders, these charming steps signal a transition between a patio floor and a flagstone path.

ABOVE A gentle slope becomes more interesting when transformed into a series of gravel terraces and fieldstone steps.

RIGHT Huge stone slabs form a simple stairway of generous proportions, just right for this large woodland garden.

TOP A simple pot on a small landing calls attention to the change in the climb's rhythm.

MIDDLE Granite blocks were used between an upper and lower lawn. Notice how the lower steps bow out toward the bottom, while the upper ones curve in the opposite direction.

BOTTOM A grand entry stairway calls for extra-wide steps and dramatic, rich-hued plantings. A collection of oversized pots and urns skillfully interrupts the stone's expanse.

OPPOSITE PAGE, TOP A naturalistic stairway fashioned from flagstone climbs past fieldstone boulders and gracefully drooping plants.

OPPOSITE PAGE, BOTTOM Bounded by thick stone walls and a wrought-iron handrail, this substantial stairway leads you securely up the hill.

Major Stairways

On a long, steep slope or in a formal landscape design, something more than a few stone steps is called for. In settings like these, the stairway itself becomes a major design statement.

Cut stone and flagstone make handsome treads, and their relatively low profile cuts an especially nice line in contrast with risers made of small stones. When such a large swath is cut through a hillside, there is often the need for a retaining wall alongside the steps, forming a raised planting bed behind the wall. Here, and in any planting scheme alongside steps, use edging plants that spill over but do not present tripping hazards. Choose plants that look good from below, too, such as those with a graceful branch structure or dangling flowers. Besides adding good looks, plants help prevent erosion.

LANDSCAPE ARCHITECT
KAREN AITKEN ON

Entry Stairways

One of the most common challenges I face is designing a comfortable stairway for a home's entry. There is nothing worse than a set of front stairs that plummets straight up or down to the front door. The best stairs curve gracefully to the entrance and are spaced at a natural gait. If possible, I repeat the stone used for the house trim or nearby garden walls to tie the whole project together."

Chapter 4

Walls, Raised Beds, and Edgings

A wall makes a strong statement in the garden. It conveys a sense of solidity and permanence, thanks in part to the nature of its materials. It also acts as a sort of frame, drawing attention to the boundaries of the property or to the edges of some feature within it. In this chapter, you'll see a wide variety of garden walls, from tall barriers of mortared boulders to low retaining walls made by simply stacking stones in layers. You'll also find plenty of ideas for adding plants that climb up, trail over, or even thrive within stone walls.

Design Considerations

A garden is really just a little piece of the natural landscape that has been set aside for cultivation. In fact, the word "garden" is derived from an Old German word meaning "enclosure." A fence or hedge can certainly enclose a space, but a stone wall carries a certain psychological heft along with its visual weight and appeal. A wall also blocks noise and wind, providing a feeling of refuge from the busy world beyond. In the case of a retaining wall, the soil itself is kept at bay.

This same sense of enclosure can be repeated within the garden: A stone wall might separate a driveway from a lawn, a patio from a pool, or a rose garden from an area where kids play. Even a low stone edging around a raised vegetable bed says, "Plants inside, path outside."

Give careful thought to the effect that the materials will have on the character of your wall. Large, dark fieldstones mortared in place make for a massive, substantial wall, while stacked sand-colored flagstones make a wall appear lighter and less imposing. Brick walls have an orderly, traditional look, while walls of stucco or painted concrete look more contemporary. Of course, you'll want your wall to relate to the architecture of your home, particularly if it is near the house.

LEFT Two stone walls perform their different functions with equal grace. The curving retaining wall follows the natural slope of the hillside, while the capped freestanding wall creates a linear boundary.

TOP RIGHT A stone pillar marks the end of a freestanding wall and provides the perfect spot for garden statuary.

RIGHT Elegant low walls of periwinkle provide a sense of enclosure without blocking the view.

Garden walls can be expensive, so it's worth researching your options thoroughly. Landscape designer Scott Colombo says, "I would almost always prefer a stone wall over a fence or hedge, but cost can become prohibitive, even on higher-end projects. Still, stone walls are by far one of the most beautiful garden elements when designed and built properly." Landscape designer Cameron Scott adds, "If you're on a budget, install a partial section in a prominent location and fill in around it with a hedge or fence."

Also remember that a wall need not be tall to have a big impact. In a small garden, it's better to keep walls fairly low; they'll offer a sense of enclosure without making you feel like a prisoner. Landscape architect Karen Aitken often uses low walls as a transition element: "These work particularly well in the front yard, also providing visual grounding for a home's façade. I find that an 18-inch-high stucco or stone wall breaks up a planting area so that a front lawn does not seem as necessary. This type of low wall acts as a boundary and adds the sense of another destination."

Freestanding Walls

A freestanding wall is simply one that is exposed on both sides, as opposed to a retaining wall, which has one face to the soil. A freestanding wall marks a boundary and may provide a sense of sheltering enclosure, but it also speaks of strong permanence. You might decide to redirect a path or expand the vegetable garden, but once a wall is built, it is likely there to stay. Give careful consideration to where it will begin and end and what course it will take. Should the wall adjoin the house and extend the footprint of the architecture? Is it needed for privacy or more as a design element? Garden designer Tara Dillard notes, "In landscaping, contrasts are always a good idea. If you have an irregular space, straight lines and right angles will work well. Curved walls will give greater interest to a rectangular or square space."

A freestanding wall creates a backdrop—actually two, one on either side—for other garden features, such as furniture, planting beds, and garden art. Depending on the orientation and location, one side may be warmed by the morning sun, while the other is shaded by a tree in the afternoon.

Walls need not be uniform expanses. A garden gate may be set into a freestanding wall, perhaps beneath an arch. In this case, the wall is framing and drawing attention to the entry point. A recirculating fountain can be built into (or mounted on) the face of a freestanding wall, with the water undulating down the stony surface or streaming unimpeded into a catch basin at the wall's base. And the top of a wall can be the perfect place to set an attractive decorative urn or bowl that will be visible from both sides.

LANDSCAPE DESIGNER
BERNARD TRAINOR ON

Freestanding Walls

I love garden walls! Freestanding walls are an essential component of the work I do. For a sense of inclusion, I'll incorporate low walls that double as garden seating, while also expressing a sense of line to accentuate the home's architecture. To invoke exclusion, a sense of security, I'll close the edges with a walled garden or a courtyard. I like the way that walls can be used to create the bones of a garden, a framework for marrying nature and structure."

OPPOSITE PAGE A low stone wall draws a line between a refined stone patio and the meadow and woodland beyond. Reinforcing the line is a strip of pebbles set into the patio floor.

TOP A tasteful mortared wall of Montana wall stone echoes the hues of nearby tree trunks and the grassy hillside beyond.

ABOVE Curved and linear freestanding walls painted melon, raspberry, and blueberry transform a simple gravel patio by surrounding it with bold form and color.

LEFT A plastered adobe wall in Southwest style is softened by a climbing rose, which also provides a shady spot for the bench. In winter, when the rose is cut back, the sun-warmed wall provides radiant heat.

BELOW A simple, elegant wall continues the colors and texture of the patio while defining a boundary and offering an appealing place to sit.

RIGHT With a cutout that mirrors the shape of a specimen tree's canopy, this whimsical mortared wall features capstones of cut bluestone.

Retaining Walls

By definition, a retaining wall is one that holds back soil. It may be a muscular structure engineered to hold back a steep hillside, perhaps requiring one or more terraces to step down the slope in sections. Where the slope is gentler, a single, more modest wall at the bottom of the hill may do the trick. On a slight incline, a retaining wall may not even be necessary, but you might want to add one just to enhance the garden space.

Wherever a retaining wall is added, look for an opportunity to include an attractive set of steps or a site-specific planting scheme. The area just above a retaining wall is ideal for plantings that billow over the edge, softening the wall while presenting flowers or foliage closer to eye level. If the wall is the right height, add a cap wide enough to make a comfortable place to sit. If the retaining wall is high, consider planting a tree or large shrub in front of it to soften its face.

LEFT This stepped rock wall gives a finished edge to the lush planting of grasses and perennials behind it.

TOP RIGHT Anchored by a massive boulder, these stacked-stone walls hold back the hillside while providing plenty of gardening opportunities in the terrace formed between them.

RIGHT This multilevel structure incorporates planting beds and two patios in a creative solution to a very steep slope on a small lot.

A few practical considerations: A steep slope may need considerable grading as part of the retaining-wall installation, and drainage issues will need to be addressed, since a wall can restrict the flow of water above and below it. If your retaining wall will need to be more than 3 feet tall, it is probably advisable to have the work done by a professional. Most communities require a building permit for any retaining wall, and a soil analysis may also be required in areas that are potentially unstable.

LEFT This elegant retaining wall features a wide, smooth cap that contrasts agreeably with the intricate texture of its face.

RIGHT The neatly fitted ashlar blocks of this wall bridge the gap between square pavers of cut stone and rustic fieldstone stairs.

BELOW LEFT A single, high retaining wall creates a sunken patio that feels distinctly separate from the nearby front porch.

BELOW RIGHT The upper walls of this terraced hillside were built from less expensive concrete blocks painted to match the more attractive—and costly—stone wall at the edge of the patio.

Dry-Stacked Walls

ABOVE A new dry-laid wall has the look of age thanks to the choice of stones encrusted with lichen and moss. The undulating height makes the wall look as if it had settled over time.

A dry-stacked wall is relatively straight-forward to build. It is constructed directly on the ground and depends solely upon gravity and friction to keep the stones in place. Of course, fitting the stones together attractively is key to creating a pleasing, unified-looking wall. Landscape designer Cameron Scott has this to say: "I'm a huge fan of dry-laid walls, not just because I find them more attractive than mortared walls, but because they continue a time-honored craft. Also, they last longer than mortared walls because they flex with the ground and allow for excellent drainage."

Freestanding

This type of wall has a broad base of large stones that are partially buried, with their flattest side up. The stones are laid in two parallel lines, with each stone tilted toward the center, creating a sort of shallow trench where the two rows meet. Rubble (small, broken pieces of stone) is used to fill the spaces between these stones, then another layer of large stones is added and filled in with rubble. The process is repeated until the wall reaches nearly the desired height. As the wall increases in height, it should slant inward from both sides, making it narrower at the top than at the base. This makes

Gabion Walls

Gabions (from the Italian word for "big cage") are large wire baskets that can be filled with stones or other materials and used as retaining walls. "Gabion walls are wonderful for areas with difficult access, and they're an affordable option for retaining large areas on a budget. You can fill them with a wide variety of materials to give different looks and character to the garden."

it more stable. Flat, broad stones, often secured with mortar, are used to cap the wall.

Retaining

A dry-stacked retaining wall leans back against the hill, holding the soil in place. First, a shallow trench slightly wider than the wall stones is filled with gravel to form a bed for the bottom layer of stones. These foundation stones are laid just below soil level, with their top surface slanted toward the bank. To ensure good drainage, a perforated drainpipe is set in gravel between the bottom layer of stones and the base of the hill. The drainpipe should be laid hole-side down, and slanted on an angle toward the area where you want the water to flow. Each succeeding layer of stones is set back slightly toward the slope. A 3-foot-high wall, for

example, should step back by a total of at least 6 inches. As stones are added, gravel is used to fill in behind the wall.

Another option for holding back a gentle, fairly stable slope is to install a simple modular retaining wall consisting of interlocking concrete blocks. These systems come in various styles, and most comprise blocks with a rough finish that more or less resembles split stone. Some versions have hollow centers that can be filled with soil and plants to help hide the wall. Modular walls are usually set on a simple gravel footing with gravel backfill and a drainpipe. The blocks come in set sizes, and they interlock to create a uniform setback against the hill.

TOP LEFT Plants that need good drainage, such as the gray-green lamb's ears in the foreground, thrive atop a dry-stacked retaining wall.

TOP RIGHT The hefty boulders in this naturalistic retaining wall give the impression of having simply tumbled into place.

ABOVE In this handsome dry-stacked wall, stones were intentionally left out here and there to form planting pockets. Lavender and geranium flourish in the terraced planting beds above.

LEFT Chalky white stones with square and rectangular faces were carefully assembled to fashion a low retaining wall.

TOP This rough wall captures the rustic charm of the property while holding back a substantial slope.

ABOVE LEFT A neatly stacked curving wall separates a path from a small grove of trees. The mortared top increases the wall's stability.

ABOVE RIGHT To accomplish the uniform horizontal seams across this wall, several thin pieces were stacked to match the height of adjoining thick slabs. Long-running vertical seams weaken a dry-stacked wall and should be avoided.

Mortared Walls

A mortared free-standing wall brings an instant look of antiquity to any garden setting.

Mortar is the "glue" used to bond stones, bricks, or concrete blocks together in a wall. Mortar recipes vary, but they typically include water, portland cement, sand, and lime. To hide the mortar and emulate the look of a dry-stacked wall, mortar between stones can be scraped back before it dries, a process known as "raking." Other types of walls, such as those built from round stones or brick, will always have visible mortar. Between bricks, a neat, uniformly thick line of mortar is the goal.

One advantage of a mortared stone wall over a dry-stacked one is that it can be built in considerably less space: A mortared wall less than 3 feet tall can be as thin as 1 foot wide, half the thickness that a dry-stacked wall of comparable height would need to be. Another advantage is that a mortared wall can be built with almost any kind of stone, even round ones that would be nearly impossible to fit together securely with dry stacking.

All mortared walls must rest on a solid concrete footing; otherwise, the joints are sure to crack as the wall settles or the soil shifts with freezes. Regional weather conditions determine the required thickness and depth of the footing, so check your local building codes.

Freestanding

A freestanding wall of mortared stone is constructed much like a dry-stacked stone wall, except the first layer of stones is laid in wet mortar atop a concrete footing. Succeeding layers of stones are trial-fitted in small batches, then dampened and set aside. Mortar is applied, and the stones are set into it, using small pieces of wood to keep stones in place until mortar can be packed in. When all the stones are in place, the wall is covered in plastic for several days to let the mortar dry slowly.

For sufficient strength, a freestanding brick wall needs to be at least two bricks thick. There are a number of patterns, called "bonds," for laying brick. Basically, the bricks are arranged on a concrete base and laid with a uniform line of mortar between them. The joints are then smoothed, and the wall brushed clean.

Concrete-block walls may not sound especially attractive, but when covered with textured stucco or painted in a favorite hue, they can be transformed into things of beauty. Stone veneer—thin flagstones attached to the wall with a coat of latex bonding and mortared into place—can also be used to dress up a concrete wall.

Retaining

To hold back a gently to moderately sloping hillside, a low wall of mortared stone may be sufficient. Built in much the same way as a mortared freestanding wall, this type of wall doesn't need to lean back into the hill for stability. Unlike a dry-stacked wall, a mortared one will not allow water to seep through it, so a drainage system—either a drainpipe behind the wall or drainage holes incorporated into the wall—is particularly important.

To hold back a steep or unstable hillside, a concrete-block retaining wall—built on a concrete pad and internally reinforced with rebar—is the best choice. Once the structural wall is complete, consider adding a veneer of stone or brick for a more pleasing look.

ABOVE Extreme variation in the shapes of the veneer stones used for this wall gives it an interesting look, like a cubist painting of squares, rectangles, and lines.

RIGHT A retaining wall of hefty stones is broken into short sections separated by planting beds. The configuration adds stability while creating the opportunity for a lovely terraced garden.

BELOW This gracefully curving mortared retaining wall holds back a moderate slope. Note the finished look provided by thin capstones.

LEFT This free-standing wall of mortared limestone has deeply recessed joints that make it appear to be dry-stacked. Curry plant and catmint thrive in planting spaces incorporated into the top of the wall.

RIGHT Brick laid in a running bond pattern makes for a sturdy wall.

BELOW River rocks and pebbles adorn this mortared retaining wall for a whimsical look.

Plants for Walls

No matter what kind of garden wall you have, you can enhance its appearance and help it look more settled by choosing the right plants to combine with it.

Spillers

Many perennials have a spreading or low mounding shape that makes them perfect for planting just above a retaining wall to soften and visually interrupt its edge. Horticulturist Baldassare Mineo suggests wall rockcress (*Arabis caucasica*), aubrieta, basket-of-gold (*Aurinia saxatilis*), low-growing bellflowers, low-growing mums like *Chrysanthemum weyrichii*, cheddar pink (*Dianthus gratianopolitanus*), creeping baby's

breath (*Gypsophila repens*), silver-edged horehound (*Marrubium rotundifolium*), trailing oreganos like *Origanum rotundifolium* 'Kent Beauty', African daisy, penstemon, dense tansy (*Tanacetum densum amani*), and *Verbena peruviania*. Landscape designer Scott Colombo adds a few of his favorites as well: Santa Barbara daisy (*Erigeron karvinskianus*), common heliotrope (*Heliotropium arborescens*), and thyme.

Some low-growing shrubs will spread or bow gracefully over the top of a wall, including bearberry (*Arctostaphylos uva-ursi*), prostrate deodar cedar (*Cedrus deodora* 'Pendula'), low-growing types of cotoneaster, *Euonymus fortunei*, sunrose (*Helianthemum nummularium*), low-growing junipers, trailing forms of lantana,

lavender, ground-cover roses, Australian bluebell creeper (*Sollya heterophylla*), and prostrate forms of rosemary such as *Rosmarinus officinalis* 'Irene'.

Climbers

When it comes to using vines on walls, there are two ways to go. Some types clamber and scramble up a wall, leaning against it rather than attaching to it firmly. Choices in this category include old favorites like clematis, sweet pea, honeysuckle, climbing roses, and nasturtium. Other types, known as clinging vines, attach themselves directly to the wall. These include plants like climbing hydrangea (*Hydrangea anomala petiolaris*), creeping fig (*Ficus pumila*), ivy, Boston ivy (*Parthenocissus tricuspidata*), and Virginia creeper (*P. quinquefolia*).

OPPOSITE PAGE Practically covered in foliage and flowers, this rock wall and flagstone path create a stunning crevice garden.

TOP LEFT The drought-tolerant plants tumbling over this stone wall invite you to stroll the path slowly, perhaps touching the large, exquisitely soft leaves of lamb's ears or enjoying the bracing fresh scent of catmint (*Nepeta*).

TOP RIGHT With California poppy spilling down and common nasturtium clambering up, this stone wall is all but hidden in late spring and summer.

BOTTOM LEFT Thriving in a South-west garden, the climbing rose 'Blaze' drapes this adobe wall with brilliant color in spring, summer, and fall.

BOTTOM RIGHT Virginia creeper puts on quite a show with its autumn colors. After the leaves have fallen in winter, an attractive tracery of stems is left to decorate the wall.

Colorful bromeliads decorate a rugged white wall. In the wild, these plants perch on rocks or trees and gain their sustenance from rain and the leaf mold that gathers around their roots.

Crevice Plants

You might think that few plants could survive the dry exposed conditions found between stones in a wall, but many do thrive in this type of austere setting. Some of Baldassare Mineo's favorite plants for tucking into stone walls are creeping calamint (*Calamintha cretica*), wild buckwheat, small thymes, dwarf cinquefoils such as *Potentilla cinerea*, small varieties of Spanish lavender (*Lavandula stoechas*), lewisia, hedgehog broom (*Erinacea anthyllis*), globe daisy, mat sea lavender (*Limonium bellidifolium*), creeping shrubby ice plant (*Ruschia pulvinaris*), smaller types of stonecrop, houseleek, and diminutive germanders such as *Teucrium marum, T. ackermannii*, and *T. cossonii majoricum*. Most of the plants in the preceding list prefer sunny or lightly shaded locations. In a very shady spot, many small ferns grow beautifully in a rock wall.

ABOVE A low retaining wall features blue-gray hen and chicks (*Echeveria*) nestled into the crevices.

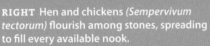

RIGHT Hen and chickens (*Sempervivum tectorum*) flourish among stones, spreading to fill every available nook.

FAR LEFT This interesting wall garden features a mass of purple bellflowers on the left, with gray hen and chickens (*Sempervivum tectorum*) just above and to the right. A small-leafed ivy forms a verdant curtain on the far right.

LEFT Ferns are tougher than they look. Many will grow readily in the crevices of a wall, and their delicate fronds in shades of fresh green contrast beautifully with stone.

Raised Beds

A series of stacked-stone raised beds mitigate a sloping property. The light-colored stones perfectly match the gravel driveway and adobe house.

Gardening in raised beds is popular for many good reasons. It's an easy solution to the problem of poor garden soil—just fill beds with organically enriched soil, which can be easily amended to suit the plants you want to grow. Raised beds warm up quickly in the spring, and they provide excellent drainage. Built into a slope, a raised bed can increase your planting area and create a level bed that is easier to work in. And raised beds are often a good solution for gardeners in wheelchairs or with back or knee problems.

When you think of raised beds, wooden frames may come to mind, but stone or brick may be an even better choice. Untreated wood rots quickly, and pressure-treated lumber may contain chemicals you definitely do not want seeping into your crop soil. A bed constructed of dry-stacked stone has a permanent look, yet it is easy to disassemble and move should you decide to change your garden's layout.

Flagstones are often chosen for constructing stacked-stone raised beds; their uniform thickness and manageable size make them easy to work with. Basically, you choose or create a level spot and mark the outlines of your planned bed's shape, then lay the largest and most irregular stones flat, with their straightest edge facing out. It's a good idea to install a liner of hardware cloth to keep out burrowing pests like gophers and moles; simply cut it to fit and pin down the edges with the first course of stone. Stack subsequent layers of flagstones until the bed is at the desired height. Fill the raised bed with soil, tamp the soil to settle it, and you're ready to plant.

Boulders also make fine walls for raised beds. If they're large enough, a single, closely fitted course of cut stones may be all you need. Or build a low dry-stacked wall from smaller boulders and add soil as you go. For a more permanent bed, install a low mortared wall of stone, bricks, or concrete blocks.

RIGHT A casual raised bed of dry-stacked boulders is easy and inexpensive to build. Thyme and other low growers fill in quickly to give an established look after just a season or two.

LEFT Stacked and mortared blocks create a tidy raised bed for herbs in this orderly garden.

BELOW Curving around the edge of a lawn, this low stone wall creates a raised bed brimming with colorful mounds and dramatically different leaf shapes. It also makes a great place to perch while Fido fetches.

RIGHT Wide flag-stones were used to cap this low wall, creating a comfortable place to sit while tending the plants in the raised bed.

A Storybook Garden

When the homeowners renovated their Middleburg, Virginia, home, adding stone arches and a new staircase to the 1830 house, they decided to reinvent the garden as well. Now, a substantial stone wall surrounding an herb parterre garden creates a storybook landscape. Raised beds are held within stone edgings, and a gravel pathway featuring a cast-iron planter leads you through the space. A fountain in the corner adds the alluring sound of splashing water.

The Elements

- **Walls.** The generously proportioned garden wall, new staircase, and arches adjoining the house are made of Virginia fieldstone.

- **Raised Beds.** Topiary boxwoods and an assortment of culinary herbs fill the raised beds, which can be accessed from the kitchen upstairs.

- **Edging.** Virginia fieldstone was mortared in place to edge the gravel path and serve as low walls for the raised beds.

- **Gravel Paths.** Pea gravel makes a wonderful sound underfoot.

- **Stone Patio.** An intimate patio awaits just outside the French doors.

- **Water Feature.** In the corner opposite the stairs sits a stone bowl that fills the garden with the magical sound of burbling water.

- **Plants.** The herbs benefit from the reflected heat of the stone edging and gravel pathway. Fragrant honeysuckle and climbing roses scramble among the stony eaves.

In some situations, you want to set off an area visually, perhaps to draw a boundary between a lawn and flower bed or a path and the garden beyond. That's where edgings come into play, and there are lots of options available. Close-set cobblestones make a neat edging and are a favorite choice among designers, including Scott Colombo and Tara Dillard. Bricks are another good choice for a tidy edge. Lay them flat between a lawn and a raised bed to form a mowing strip, or stand them on end side by side, half buried, to make a more vertical boundary. Small boulders make a nice edging, especially alongside a gravel path, where they keep the loose material in place. Basalt columns can be laid on their sides to make striking edgings, and recycled concrete curbs are just the right shape too. Choose a more formal edging material near the house, but something more casual farther out in the garden. And remember that edgings do not necessarily have to be solid. Even widely spaced stones can mark a boundary that's easy for the eye to determine.

OPPOSITE PAGE Installed along with the flagstone path, this stone edging is high enough to form a visual border, but low enough to allow plants to billow over.

TOP This double edging includes a line of mortared bricks and a gravel strip alongside a lawn with inset pavers. A lawn mower can pass over all of these elements, making mowing easier.

RIGHT Cut-stone pavers make a handsome edging between a gravel path and a planting bed featuring a partially buried boulder.

LEFT Small river-washed boulders define an artistically swirling garden feature that is part path, part raised bed.

TOP A wide stone edging continues the line and color of the adjoining wall and makes an easy job of mowing the lawn next to the planting bed.

ABOVE The curving line of this bed, crisply outlined by a low edging, contrasts nicely with the right angles of the cut-stone patio.

Chapter 5

Boulders, Stone Accents, and Rock Gardens

Stones not only make sturdy garden paths and structures, they also serve beautifully as decorative accents and artistic elements in the landscape. A simple group of artfully arranged boulders surrounded by ornamental grasses and wildflowers can transform an empty corner of the backyard into something far more interesting and evocative. Garden accents made of stone, whether carved or assembled, combine the rugged look of nature with the touch of the artist's hand. And rock gardens, where the stones create the framework for a special kind of planting scheme, possess a charm that only increases with closer inspection.

Design Considerations

Recycled granite plinths and a concrete urn provide contrast to a sweep of lavender.

With its heft, durability, and natural beauty, stone is an ideal choice for garden ornaments, perhaps because it provides such a striking contrast to the living plants surrounding it. While a collection of carved statues of people and animals can look out of place, even pretentious or silly, a simple stone marker at the beginning of a path possesses a quiet dignity. Landscape architect Karen Aitken says, "I prefer boulders to formal sculpture, which can be difficult to incorporate into a garden because of scale. Most sculptures need a lot of space around them to be fully enjoyed, and many home gardens just don't have enough room." Even utilitarian objects, like benches, birdbaths, and planting containers, seem more settled in the garden when they're made of stone.

When placing any stone element, take careful note of how it fits in the landscape. A stone sundial might take center stage in a circular herb garden, while a group of boulders casually arranged might make more sense near the bottom of a slope. Surround stone elements with plants to make them look more natural in the setting. Be sure to choose plants of appropriate scale; there's no point in creating a beautiful arrangement if it winds up hidden by foliage. The most effective display comes when the stone element is partially obscured by greenery or displayed against a solid backdrop of plants. The fine foliage of many grasses and ferns looks particularly lovely against a stone surface.

Rock gardens are usually meant to mimic nature, but you should feel free to be creative in your combinations of plants and stone. A dry strip alongside the driveway might be just the spot for a collection of drought-tolerant plants set among stones and surrounded by gravel.

LEFT A stone sphere like this one can be moved about the garden, drawing attention to different parts of the landscape at different times of the year.

TOP RIGHT In this miniature landscape, the upright stone echoes the shape of the columnar evergreen on the far left, forming a sort of bracket around the featured dwarf shrub.

BOTTOM RIGHT Baby's tears creeps up the rough surface of a boulder. Setting stones in quick-growing ground covers helps give them a settled look in the garden.

Boulders

Depending on their shape and how they're placed, boulders can serve many different purposes in a garden. Wide, low stones may be seen as anchors, perhaps nestled beneath the boughs of a low-branching tree. Tall thin stones might serve as sentinels flanking the entrance to a path. As landscape architect Karen Aitken points out, "Boulders can be a unifying element in an informal design, serving as turning points in a walk or lawn edge or even acting as camouflage for irrigation, hose bibs, and electrical boxes."

Generally, boulders look best if they're placed the way they would appear in the natural landscape. Consider taking a drive or hike to observe stone. In nature, you'll find like kinds of stones grouped together, so follow that example if you're after a natural look. Outcroppings of boulders usually run in parallel bands, so when you're placing several stones together, line them up so that any stratification runs in the same direction. If layers aren't obvious, position the stones so that their top surfaces all tilt at the same angle. Several small stones can be made to look like pieces of a huge boulder by grouping them fairly close together, with their most jagged edges facing up. If a boulder breaks apart while you're installing it, so much the better; just leave the pieces with the broken seams parallel.

Large river-washed boulders form a crescent around a circular pond fed by a stone runnel. The smooth stones seem to settle the water feature into the landscape.

Boulders are rarely found sitting on top of the ground; they typically rise out of the ground, often with just a tip or one or two faces showing. To get this effect in your garden, bury stones up to their widest point or with a third to a half beneath the soil. If one side of the boulder has moss or looks weathered, that side should face up. Garden designer Tara Dillard advises studying each stone carefully: "Boulders speak. They tell you which is their front, top, and side face, how deeply they should be buried. An old Chinese saying gives good advice for placing two stones: One, the male, should reach toward the sky and the other, the female, should lie with the earth."

Long thin boulders can be placed flat, perhaps serving as a bench or a low wall, or planted upright as a vertical accent. As landscape designer Scott Colombo notes, "Tall columnar boulders can be spectacular in the garden, but their placement should make sense and not be willy-nilly. A natural-looking arrangement might include one upright column and a couple of large flat boulders that double as benches." For a stone column to stand securely, about one-fourth of its height should be below ground. Dig a hole that matches the shape of the stone's base so it will be stable and add smaller rocks into the hole to lock the boulder into position. For very tall columns (over 6 feet), set the stone on a concrete pad in a hole that is one-third the length of the stone and three times its width. Fill in with crushed gravel, tamp it down firmly every 6 inches or so, then add 4 inches of topsoil.

Practical Points

When you're ready to shop for boulders, visit a stone yard and take along a tape measure and camera. You'll probably find yourself attracted to one or two types of stones. Photograph them and take an approximate measure of their dimensions, then return home and think about how they'll look on your property (remember that they'll be partially buried). You can fashion stand-ins from garbage bags filled with newspaper to help you decide on placement.

If the boulders you choose are too large for you to handle yourself, check with the stone yard about delivery. They may offer this service or be able to suggest a local company that specializes in the work. If the boulders aren't too large, hired workers may handle the delivery and placement, using a hand truck. Forklifts can fit through gates as narrow as 6 feet. For larger stones, a boom truck or crane may be required. Be sure to plan on where the stones will be unloaded, preferably not on a concrete driveway (though wooden pallets may offer some protection) or above a septic tank. The delivery crew can help you position stones, but decide where the stones will be placed and dig holes for them beforehand. You'll likely be paying for the crew's service by the hour.

If you'll be moving the stones yourself, follow these guidelines to avoid injuring your back. First, roll, drag, tip, or pry heavy stones whenever possible. Wear leather gloves and sturdy boots, and be sure to stand to the side of a rock as you're moving it (so that if it rolls, it doesn't roll onto you). To use a wheelbarrow, tip it on its side and roll the stone in; then brace your foot against the wheel and tip the wheelbarrow upright. (Barrows are better for relatively small stones, since a large boulder can easily shift and tip the barrow over.) Or use a garden cart or hand truck. You can also place a boulder on plywood and roll it on a series of four or five dowels, continually moving the rear dowel to the front as the plywood moves forward. If you do need to lift a heavy stone, always bend your knees, keep your back straight, grasp the stone firmly, then straighten your knees, keeping your elbows close to your sides.

CLOCKWISE FROM NEAR RIGHT Echoing the color of the house and contrasting with its right angles, a trio of smooth boulders sits amid soft, flowing grasses.

Forming a sculpture garden reminiscent of Easter Island, these monolithic stones rise as high as 7 feet. The designer chose to leave their bases nearly bare to accentuate their unusual, towering form.

A single boulder looks right at home among low-growing and upright sedums and a drought-tolerant shrub (Arbutus unedo). The stone tip directs the eye toward a decorative metal piece mounted on the wall.

Basalt columns are natural formations resulting from cooling lava that fractured vertically. The columns shown here were drilled to make fountains, but they are dramatic with or without the flowing water.

Low, wide boulders seem to float on an ocean of blue flowers, with a splash of ornamental grass evoking a cresting wave. Taller, denser plants might obscure the stones completely.

Stone Accents

Boulders have an undeniable appeal simply as "natural sculptures," but there are many other ways to use stone to enhance your garden. Some stones can serve as functional pieces, such as a boulder with a depression in the top that forms a shallow pool just right for a birdbath. A short column might be just the right size for a stone table base or single-person bench. And, of course, stone can be carved into just about any shape, from a simple block or sphere to an elaborate, realistic piece of statuary.

Stone may also be used as a base upon which other features, like sundials or lanterns, are displayed. Such a base may be carved from a single stone or constructed from smaller rocks.

Whether it's a recycled piece of concrete curb, an antique architectural fragment, or an original construction of stacked flagstone, a decorative stone feature can bring character and personal style to your garden.

OPPOSITE PAGE
A pair of egg-shaped river rocks nest on a single cobblestone surrounded by purple sweet alyssum (*Lobularia maritima*), pink and orange twinspurs (*Diascia* hybrids), and lime thyme (*Thymus* x *citriodorus*).

ABOVE Rising from a luxuriant expanse of grasses, this Chinese lantern of carved stone seems to give order and form to the space around it.

RIGHT The clean lines of these granite birdbaths make them suitable for a garden design of almost any style.

OPPOSITE PAGE A massive old millstone has earned its retirement, resting upright alongside a patio where it echoes the shape of the table.

TOP LEFT A stone sphere rests in a niche at the top of a limestone wall.

TOP RIGHT This porous lava boulder has a large open space on top, so the gardener added soil and a *Euphorbia myrsinites.* Delicate Kenilworth ivy *(Cymbalaria muralis)* and purple Serbian bellflower *(Campanula poscharskyana)* creep up the sides.

BOTTOM LEFT A multipurpose stone structure houses a mailbox and a newspaper receptacle, and serves as a signpost and lantern base too.

BOTTOM RIGHT Glowing in peaceful repose, a stone face rests on a pool of beach glass.

Stone Benches

Every garden needs places to sit, and a simple bench made from a slab of stone, a low boulder, or an assemblage of stone makes a welcome destination. Stone benches are not as comfortable as wooden ones, so place them where you might want to sit for just a few moments, perhaps to admire a view or rest briefly along a path. Since stone can get uncomfortably hot, site your stone bench in shade, or, at least, where it will get afternoon shade. A bench nestled against plants feels more comfortable than one exposed on all sides. You can set your bench directly in soil, but placing it in a stone or gravel base will help ensure its stability.

A low boulder might be just the right height and shape for a single seat, but a bench for two requires a flat surface between 4 and 5 feet long and a seat depth of about 20 inches. A slab with these dimensions set atop two stones buried 6 inches deep makes a steady, stable bench. The top of a bench should be about 16 to 18 inches above ground level.

TOP Thick cushions and assorted pillows make this stone bench almost as comfortable and stylish as an indoor sofa.

BOTTOM A stone bench is just the right height for sitting to inspect the gorgeous blooms of oakleaf hydrangea *(Hydrangea quercifolia).*

OPPOSITE PAGE, TOP This informal sitting place is simply the corner of a low wall built from various types of stone.

OPPOSITE PAGE, BOTTOM Angling out from a stone wall, this stone slab serves equally well as a bench and a place to display a handsome plum-colored jar.

LANDSCAPE ARCHITECT
CRAIG BERGMANN ON

Council Rings

A council ring is a low stone wall built around a circular patio, with a single opening for entry and capstones wide enough to serve as a bench. Midwest landscape architect Jens Jensen (1860–1951) used council rings extensively in his designs, promoting them as quiet spots for conversation, reading, or personal reflection. He sited them carefully in wooded areas with a bluff, overlook, or other point of interest. A fire ring was often included in the center for that age-old favorite activity of gathering around a campfire to tell scary stories or tall tales."

Rock Gardens

Classic rock gardens combine meticulously placed stones with dwarf conifers and tiny alpine plants to create a sort of miniature mountain scene. More casual rock gardens, sometimes called rockeries, include a wider variety of plants and may take many different forms, from a collection of succulents tucked around stones to a rocky slope dotted with grasses and small daisies. But all rock gardens depend on the naturally appealing combination of rocks and plants that grow well among them. The traditional composition is two-fifths rock and three-fifths plants—a good formula to use regardless of the type of rock garden you wish to make.

Creating a Simple Rock Garden

If you'd like to experiment with a small rock garden, there are a few simple versions you can try. The basic idea is to arrange stones in a way that creates pockets of soil—or at least open areas between stones—for the plants. Most rock-garden plants require excellent drainage. For best results, choose a spot on sloping ground or create a mound, and provide fast-draining soil.

To mimic a natural rocky outcropping, install a few good-sized boulders securely into a hillside, with smaller stones of various sizes scattered around them and piled at the base of the hill as if they'd broken loose and tumbled down. An arrangement like this creates plenty of planting areas.

Another fairly quick and easy variation on the rock-garden theme is a slab garden. For this compact garden feature, choose a large stone that can be split into three or four slabs (think of thick slices of bread); have the rock yard do the splitting for you. Back in your garden, piece the slabs back together, but leave gaps of at least a few inches between them. Pack the gaps with a layer of gravel topped by fast-draining soil mix, and plant between and around the pieces.

Building a Scree

For a more advanced rock garden in the alpine style, consider building a scree to provide the necessary perfect drainage. In nature, a scree is a pile of flaked or fragmented stone found at the base of cliffs or on mountain ridges. Choose a sunny, breezy spot, preferably on a slope. Dig the entire area 18 inches deep, and group several boulders in it near the top of the slope. For a natural look, position the boulders so that their grain runs in the same direction and their tops tilt at the same angle. Next, spread a 6-inch-thick layer of drainage material, which can be a mixture of half gravel and half sand—even rocks and broken pieces of brick and old concrete will do. Then set a few more large stones on top and fill in the area with a fast-draining soil mix: A good mixture is equal parts pea gravel, coarse sand, garden soil, and organic compost.

Finish the scree by spreading a layer of 1 to 2 inches of gravel (choose gravel that is ¾-inch diameter or smaller) over the area. When you are ready to plant, carefully clear back the gravel from the planting spot, and place the plants so that the top of the rootball is slightly above ground, then push the gravel around the crown of the plant.

OPPOSITE PAGE A gentle slope set with boulders from a local source creates an ideal location for a rock garden. Plants spill onto the gravel path and occasionally set seed in it.

TOP LEFT Soft gray stonecrop (*Sedum spathulifolium* 'Cape Blanco') flows like lava around these well-placed boulders. Bright pink *Aubrieta* and lemon-yellow draba brighten the scene.

TOP RIGHT Tufts of pink-flowered thrift (*Armeria maritima*) and a creeping blue speedwell (*Veronica prostrata*) hug a rocky ledge.

ABOVE Spring is often the showiest time of year for rock gardens, when many alpine plants bloom profusely. This classic example is planted in partial shade.

LEFT Here's an inventive way to include a rock garden on your property. Build a wide, deep stairway and leave plenty of pockets to fill with soil and plants. Ascending the stairs, you'll get a close-up view of your plant collection.

OPPOSITE PAGE, TOP A dwarf lupine shows off purple flowers that seem all the more brilliant among the sand-colored stones.

OPPOSITE PAGE, MIDDLE The vibrant violet-blue flowers of *Campanula saxifraga* practically cover the plant in late spring or early summer. Its long taproot finds moisture deep in crevices between stones.

OPPOSITE PAGE, BOTTOM A low rectangular planter picks up the pink in the leaf tips of a blue-green hen and chicks (*Echeveria*).

Rock-Garden Plants

Many types of plants can be used in rock gardens, but there are a few basic requirements. They should be small enough so that they don't overwhelm the stones. Well-behaved plants that creep along the ground or grow into tidy mounds are desirable in a smaller rock garden. For larger compositions, somewhat bigger plants are fine—just keep scale in mind. Choose plants that thrive in well-drained conditions. If your rock garden is in a sunny spot, plants should be able to handle the reflected heat of stone. Avoid formal-looking plants like roses and camellias; they seem out of place in the naturalistic setting of a rock garden.

Dwarf conifers are classic choices. Look for dwarf varieties of false cypress (*Chamaecyparis*), juniper, spruce, fir, pine, and hemlock. Some look like nearly perfect miniatures; others grow into small, dense globe shapes; and still others form creeping mats or have long, drooping branches. Most grow quite slowly, so plan on filling in around them with bulbs or small perennials while they attain some size.

Among the many small shrubs suitable for a rock garden are dwarf or prostrate types of cotoneaster, daphne, heath (*Erica*), heather (*Calluna*), *Hebe*, shrubby cinquefoil (*Potentilla fruticosa*), and rhododendron.

Flowering perennials seem particularly at home snuggled up to stone. Look for small-growing types of yarrow, stonecress, lady's mantle, *Alyssum*, rock jasmine (*Androsace*), columbine, thrift, aster, pinks, bellflower, cranesbill (*Erodium*), *Euphorbia myrsinites*, geranium, candytuft, *Iris pumila*, phlox, *Silene*, speedwell, and thyme. Succulents like stonecrop and houseleek look great among stones, in or out of bloom, as do many ornamental grasses.

Container Rock Gardens

To make a miniature rock garden for the patio, start with a container 12 to 18 inches across and at least 6 inches deep, with an adequate drainage hole. Fill with fast-draining potting soil, and position a couple of interesting stones 4 to 6 inches wide and tall to create a crevice for a spider-web *Sempervivum* or a tiny stonecrop like *Sedum acre* 'Aureum'. For the main plant, choose one with tiny foliage and a natural bonsai look, like a dwarf Chinese elm (*Ulmus parvifolia* 'Hokkaido') or a miniature hemlock cultivar such as *Tsuga canadensis* 'Jacqueline Verkade'. Filler plants might include yellow-flowered *Alyssum tortuosum*, pink rock jasmine (*Androsace sempervivoides*), blue *Globularia repens*, or a miniature thyme."

The delicate fronds of ferns make a lovely contrast with rocks.

Bulbs for the rock garden include petite forms of crocus, cyclamen, snowdrop, snowflake, grape hyacinth, and narcissus, including the charming dwarf daffodils.

Although rock-garden plants need soil that drains well, the soil must also hold nutrients. Whether your soil is sandy or clay, the addition of organic matter such as aged bark will be beneficial. Avoid peat moss, as it holds too much moisture. For extra porosity, you can incorporate small pebbles or gravel into the soil. These materials also make an excellent mulch. Water your rock garden deeply but not too frequently, and go easy on the fertilizer.

TOP Cracked and weathered, these stones look like they might have been in place for eons. The wave-raked gravel gives the impression of constant motion.

MIDDLE This Japanese-inspired design features a large standing boulder and several supporting stones placed to suggest a stream. Smoother stones were chosen for placement within the "water."

BOTTOM Raked into a checkerboard grid, this gravel field offers a thoughtful contrast to the serenity of a single boulder and its surrounding ripples.

OPPOSITE PAGE A weeping cherry tree rises from a green mound behind this impressive garden of gravel and stone.

Japanese-Style Rock Gardens

Gardens in the Japanese style often place a special emphasis on stone. Rocks are carefully chosen for their individual character, with rough weather-beaten boulders preferred for their appearance of great age. These are arranged in sculptural groupings, where each stone relates to its neighbors in an aesthetically pleasing way—the goal, a sort of balanced asymmetry. Rugged, upright boulders may be used to suggest mountains, while lower, smoother ones evoke islands. Gravel is used to represent water.

For designs that incorporate plants, the focus is on form rather than on colorful flowers, although rhododendrons, azaleas, and camellias may contribute seasonal flourishes. A low mound might feature a dwarf pine or a small graceful tree such as a Japanese maple or pagoda dogwood (*Cornus alternifolia*), underplanted with low-growing plants like stonecrop, dwarf mondo grass (*Ophiopogon japonicus* 'Kyoto Dwarf'), or pachysandra.

Dry gravel gardens, or Zen gardens as they're sometimes called, feature a carefully thought-out arrangement of boulders on a sea of gravel. The gravel is often raked to suggest waves or ripples around the stones, although abstract patterns are also an option. Choose a sharp-edged gravel between ⅛ and ½ inch in size, and look for a tan or salt-and-pepper color, as pure white is too glaring. Chicken grit (⅛ inch) and turkey grit (⅜ inch) are available at feed stores; both are good choices for a raked-gravel garden. Specialty rakes are available for creating the ripples, or you can use a garden fork or an old rake with every other tine removed.

Laid-Back Rock Gardens

Case Study

THIS PAGE With its bright green, red-tipped leaves, *Echeveria agavoides* 'Lipstick' takes center stage in this circular rock garden. Supporting players are golden-variegated rockcress (*Arabis ferdinandi-coburgi* 'Variegata'), miniature creeping thyme, and various colorful varieties of houseleek.

OPPOSITE PAGE, LEFT A narrow bed along the top of a wall approximates the stony outcroppings preferred by these rugged plants. Once they're established, they'll need only occasional watering during the driest part of the summer.

OPPOSITE PAGE, RIGHT Tucked between the wall and several types of stone, this powdery blue *Dudleya* is guaranteed the perfect drainage it requires.

The author's garden is located in Sausalito, California; and at a few feet above sea level, it's hardly an ideal spot for a traditional alpine rock garden. But that doesn't mean a rock garden is out of the question. Two casual areas featuring succulents thrive in the landscape. One is a circular rock garden 4 feet in diameter and situated just across a path from a bench, allowing for close-up viewing of the jewel-like plants. The second space, a narrow strip 12 feet long and just 18 inches wide, was planted above a concrete-and-stone retaining wall that is over half a century old. Here too you can view the plants easily by walking right up to the wall.

The Elements

■ **Stone Circle.** Small boulders of locally quarried stone were used for the circular bed, which was originally dug 2 feet deep and filled with stone rubble, sand, and compost. A few pieces of amethyst were added to sparkle in the sun.

■ **Strip Garden.** For the edging along the narrow bed, round river stones salvaged from another project were put to use. This area was already filled with extremely fast-draining, sandy soil, so only compost was added.

■ **Gravel.** Pami pebbles create a colorful gravel mulch in both rock gardens, visually tying together the nearby areas.

■ **Succulents.** Various succulents thrive in this garden, where winter temperatures rarely fall below freezing and summer heat is moderated by a foggy marine layer. *Echeveria*, houseleek (*Sempervivum*), *Crassula*, stonecrop, and *Dudleya* are well suited here.

■ **Perennials.** Low-growing perennials among the succulents include rockcress, miniature creeping thyme, and purple sweet alyssum.

Water Features

Water and stone are opposites in many ways, yet somehow they are always compatible. Water, clear and reflective when still, can make fantastic patterns in motion, creating sounds that can be soothing or stimulating. Stone, solid and opaque, exemplifies quiet strength. Stone can be a vessel for water, setting its course in a stream or holding it in a simple bowl. Water affects stone, darkening its color and eventually wearing it down. A water feature in the garden—whether a splashing fountain, a still pond surrounded by mossy boulders, or a dry creekbed that merely suggests moisture—focuses our attention on the elemental pairing of water and stone.

Design Considerations

A water feature is one of the surest ways to draw people into the garden. They might see it first from indoors, noticing the sparkle of a sunlit fountain. Or they might hear a low burbling in the backyard and feel drawn to find its source. When they find the water, they'll almost certainly pause to study it—what designers call a "garden moment."

If you happen to have a natural stream or pond on your property, you already have the perfect focal point for your garden design. On the other hand, creating a large water feature that *looks* natural can be tricky. If you have a sloping yard, a stream might look right meandering down the hill,

especially if you can disguise the uphill source. A flat place where water would naturally collect is needed for a realistic pond, but don't choose the lowest spot in the garden; when the rains come, you could have problems with flooding. To help make any water feature look more natural, design it with plenty of irregularity, such as varied edgings around a pool or several different-size river stones in a stream. Surround it with plants to make it look believable.

For a small suburban lot, however, you may be better off treating your water feature as an introduced design element rather than trying to make it look as if it has always been there. Whether it's a stone water bowl, a concrete fountain, or a small watercourse running in a straight line across a patio, a crafted feature can be seen as a celebration of water for its own sake. If there is other stone work in your garden, try to integrate the water feature with similar materials so it doesn't look like an afterthought.

Whatever type you choose, consider locating the water feature where you can see it from indoors so you can enjoy it in all seasons. Think about how much light will fall on it. Water sparkles beautifully in the sun, and fish, as well as many water plants, need at least half a day of sunlight in order to thrive. A small water bowl placed beneath a tree reflects the dappled light above. You may wish to add lighting so that you can see the water feature at night, but don't get carried away. Bright spotlights can look particularly garish when trained on water.

Be sure to place your water feature where people will have access to the water itself, so they can touch it or at least study closely how it moves or reflects. Even the air around a water feature is different—cooler and moister—so take advantage of that, perhaps placing a bench nearby among a group of ferns that will look particularly robust in the increased humidity.

LANDSCAPE DESIGNER
BERNARD TRAINOR ON

Water Features

Water features are especially effective in areas with little rainfall. Gardens designed with drought-tolerant landscapes can look a bit dry, and even a small fountain has a refreshing, cooling effect. We often place the water feature near a seating area, or anywhere we want to create an oasis where people are sure to gather."

OPPOSITE PAGE A round reflecting pool makes an inviting focal point on this peaceful flagstone patio. The *faux bois* (false wood) furniture is made from a concrete mixture and sculpted to look like wood.

TOP LEFT Is it real or is it constructed? Years of experience are needed to be able to create and install a stream and waterfall that are this convincing.

TOP RIGHT A recirculating fountain made from stacked flagstone brings welcome splash and sparkle to this dry garden, without using much water.

ABOVE Cut-stone coping makes an elegant edge for this water garden. Grasses and other narrow-leafed plants look right at home around the edges. The small burbling fountain keeps the water moving.

Fountains

Like a natural geyser, this splashy garden fountain adds excitement you can see, hear, and feel. Numerous strips of flagstone, set on edge and wedged closely together, form the fountain's base.

A fountain, by definition, moves water, tossing it into the air or sending it tumbling over an edge. Besides being irresistible to watch, moving water can make a variety of appealing sounds, from the splash of a spray fountain to the burble or drip of a spilling bowl on a bed of stones. Even against a background of traffic noise, these sounds stand out and refocus our attention.

All fountains have the same basic parts: a bowl where gravity takes the water, a submerged pump for lifting the water, and an outlet pipe that leads from the pump to the fountain device such as a spray nozzle or a spout. To power your fountain, you'll need to connect it directly (not with an extension cord) to a ground-fault-protected outlet with a waterproof cover, concealing the fountain cord and outlet from view. Solar-powered fountain sets are available, some with a separate solar panel and some with the panel incorporated into the bowl. Disguise the "works" by screening the panel and cord with plants, for instance, or by placing an in-bowl solar fountain slightly above eye level so that you can't see the technology inside.

Locate your fountain out of the wind so that the water doesn't blow away. And be sure to choose a fountain that you find attractive even when it's not running.

Types of Fountains

Though they all share the same basic components, recirculating fountains can move water in a variety of ways, for quite different effects.

SPILL FOUNTAINS appear to be perpetually overflowing, with the water simply tumbling down the sides of the fountain into the catch basin. If the fountain's surface is smooth, the water can be almost undetectable, almost like a

shimmering gloss. A rougher surface produces a livelier dance of light.

SPRAY OR SPLASH FOUNTAINS shoot water upward in various patterns, from large upright columns to lacy sprays or even just bubbling or frothing from the top.

WALL FOUNTAINS pour water from a spout mounted on a vertical surface into a catch basin below. The spout may be a simple spigot or a horizontal ledge that creates a small waterfall.

TOP LEFT A couple of round stones set atop this fountain constrict the trajectory of the water, making it gurgle rather than splash. For a more exuberant display, the stones could be rearranged or removed.

ABOVE LEFT This Japanese *tsukubai* (hand-washing station) includes a bamboo waterspout and an overflowing stone bowl set on river stones.

TOP RIGHT Jutting from a curving blue wall, this stone ledge shapes the cascading water into a transparent curtain.

ABOVE RIGHT Fashioned from drilled concrete disks, this small, simple fountain has a dignified, antique look.

The centerpiece of this elegant garden is a massive fountain of carved stone set in a circular pool. A surrounding ring of dark cobblestones lets you stand close enough to touch the rippling flow.

TOP Rising from a stone-lined pond, an oversized jet-black bowl makes a dramatic focal point. The water splashes twice—once in the bowl and once in the pond—to make a distinct, rhythmic sound.

ABOVE LEFT A handsome concrete fountain, filled with stones and bubbling water, sits serenely in a sea of lavender.

ABOVE RIGHT This minimalist fountain comprises a concrete cube, black pebbles, and a modest spray of water.

Pondless Fountains

Among the most popular garden fountains are in-ground "pondless" types, where the catch basin and pump are below ground level, covered by a grate that is hidden under decorative stones. The outlet pipe might emerge between pebbles, creating a burble or spray that appears to be coming from an underground source. Or the pipe might travel through a boulder that has been drilled for the purpose, so water appears to be flowing from the stone itself. The main advantage of a pondless fountain is that you don't have an aboveground body of water that might attract unwanted pests or present a danger to toddlers.

ABOVE Water slides smoothly down the surface of a spherical stone fountain, causing it to shimmer in the sunlight.

RIGHT This handsome contemporary fountain was fashioned from a monolithic concrete cube set into a cutout in the deck. The rough stones at the base make a subtle but effective contrast with the fountain's sleek lines.

Streams and Waterfalls

A moving stream incorporating one or more waterfalls is one of the most dramatic features you can add to your garden. It's like a course of kinetic energy that runs right through the property.

Streams

Artificial streams are built with waterproof liners of PVC or rubber, and, like recirculating fountains, they depend on a pump to bring the water uphill. (For reliable water flow, your stream needs to fall about 1 inch for every 8 feet of length.) A stream may connect two artificial ponds, or one or both ends can be concealed water reservoirs.

If your property slopes, you have a much better chance of creating a natural-looking stream, especially if you can make its origin look convincing. A pile of boulders in the middle of a flat yard won't do the trick, but a stream that appears to curve from behind a group of evergreens at the back of the property might feel right. If possible, design your stream to meander

along your property's natural drainage course, and line it with stones of all sizes, from boulders to pebbles. For a placid meadow stream, choose smooth river rocks and keep the banks at about the same level. To evoke a splashing mountain stream, use jagged stones and make the banks uneven, perhaps creating narrow falls here and there.

If you're not going for a natural look, you have even more options. A formal rill, or water channel, can cut across a patio, bisect a set of stairs, or even connect two pools.

Waterfalls

Waterfalls can be incorporated into a naturalistic stream at any point, though a large fall usually looks most natural emptying into the base pool (the bottom of the water course). For any type of waterfall, give careful consideration to the lip, where the water spills over the edge. A flat, wide surface will create a broad sheet of water; two close-set stones or a small spigot will channel the flow into a narrow stream. Also consider whether the water will fall unimpeded or rush down the face of the stones, sparkling and splashing as it goes.

The sound your waterfall makes will depend on where the water lands. A single stream can be almost silent as it slips into a pond not far below, but a long drop onto pebbles or irregular boulders makes quite a splash. You also may be able to adjust the pump to make the water move at different speeds. Experiment with different arrangements to get the sound you want.

Several types of ready-made waterfalls are available. Some are single-piece liners with steps molded in, and others may include a holding basin, filtration system, and spillway. When set into a hillside and surrounded by stone, these can look fairly realistic, and they're easy to install.

LEFT This hillside property is the ideal setting for an artificial stream, complete with steep rocky banks and a series of small waterfalls.

BOTTOM LEFT A stone footbridge makes it easy to cross this dramatic man-made stream. It takes a few years for plants to mature to this degree, but when they do, the stream looks completely natural.

BOTTOM RIGHT Casual and charming, this "water wall" allows a trickle of water to dance upon the stones as it moves from the upper to the lower pool.

OPPOSITE PAGE, TOP Streaming from a stacked-stone sauna, this waterfall makes an inviting splash that is guaranteed to attract visitors.

OPPOSITE PAGE, BOTTOM This impressive water sculpture was carved from natural stones and set against the hillside to send a splashing cascade into the pool.

LANDSCAPE ARCHITECT
CRAIG BERGMANN ON

Streams and Waterfalls

To make a stream or waterfall seem more natural, always be sure to completely conceal all of the liner material; one piece of exposed black rubber can completely spoil the illusion. Use stones of many different sizes, not just boulders and pebbles. And when it comes to waterfalls, don't get carried away with the height. The taller the waterfall, the more artful the stone stack must be in order to get a pleasing effect."

Dry Creekbeds

One popular and useful "water feature" may not always include water. Dry creekbeds take the form of a creek or stream, with a meandering course and stone-studded banks, but they only suggest the presence of flowing water. Some are constructed to be realistic, with steep banks and smooth river rocks of different sizes. Others are more stylized, perhaps with uniform, flat black pebbles representing water that flows around sculptural boulders.

A thoughtfully sited dry creekbed can also help drainage, turning into a wet creekbed during rainstorms. According to landscape designer Bernard Trainor: "Used honestly, dry creekbeds denote where water would flow if it were there. They should follow the topography of a property, leading toward a low point where water would naturally be diverted. They also make good opportunities for adding other features, like a small bridge or a seating area located where you look across to the other bank."

Landscape architect Craig Bergmann notes, "Dry streams are great for textural contrast and are often used to improve drainage in flat gardens." And garden designer Tara Dillard agrees on their usefulness: "Whenever you have a drainage problem, consider installing a dry streambed before going to the trouble and expense of a French drain."

To make your dry creekbed's course look as natural as possible, remember that water always follows the path of least resistance, slipping downhill and curving around even the slightest rise. Dig a shallow channel along the planned course, and use the excavated soil to create low hills, or berms, on either side. Natural creeks widen where they bend, perhaps curving around a large boulder

OPPOSITE PAGE This natural-looking dry creekbed is edged with fast-growing ornamental grasses and orange-flowered torch lily.

RIGHT Large boulders jut from the banks of this dry creekbed, just as they might in a rushing mountain stream.

BOTTOM Paddle-leafed *Opuntia* plants appear to be leaning in for a drink from this stylized creekbed. Even the suggestion of water creates a powerful impact in a desert landscape.

and creating a shallow beach downstream. Large boulders stay in the middle of the stream, while smaller ones are washed to the sides and become half-buried in silt.

Once your dry creekbed is completed, add plants along the banks to help blend it into the landscape and capture the lush look of a natural waterway. Grasses and other plants with thin, reedlike leaves look particularly natural alongside a stream.

Ponds

ABOVE This fanciful pond features a small waterfall and underwater lighting. The stone wall spirals and undulates along the large garden pond.

Whether it's a small, naturalistic pond filled with fish and plants or a formal reflecting pool as still and shiny as a mirror, your pond can be made more appealing with the incorporation of stone. An aboveground pond might be contained within low stone walls that double as seating. Stone makes a fine edging for a pond, and a few boulders placed in the water evoke stony islands.

If you're thinking of adding a pond to your garden, there are a few practical points to consider. First is safety. If you or your neighbors have very

young children or if kids will be visiting your garden frequently, be sure to restrict access to the pool or pond area with fencing and a locking gate. Also, since water and electricity can be dangerous in combination, be sure all wiring for pumps or lighting meets electrical code requirements. For any pond or pool deeper than 3 feet, you should check with your local building department about necessary permits.

To make your pond blend into the garden better, plant one side of it with reeds or grasses—plants that naturally grow alongside water. You may also

ABOVE Two waterfalls—one tumbling down a rocky bank, the other streaming from a tipped urn—grace this raised pond. A broadly capped wall makes a good spot for leaning over and looking into the water.

LEFT This contemporary pond makes great use of a small space, incorporating a comfortable wooden bench at the edge of a bluestone patio.

RIGHT A copper bowl is shaped to drop three streams of water into the lower pool of this romantic entry garden.

want to add stepping-stones atop concrete footings that allow you to walk across the pond. Or add boulders to the middle of a pond to form a sort of island; setting the boulders on extra layers of liner material or sand will keep them from damaging the pond liner or shell.

Another thing to remember is that ponds attract wildlife, which seems like a good thing when you're watching dragon-flies cavort above the water lilies, but not so great when you discover that raccoons have made a midnight snack of your goldfish. Songbirds and butterflies will come, but so too may herons and other birds of prey. Mosquitoes will breed in standing water unless it is treated; natural, organic products are available for this purpose. Or you can stock your pond with goldfish and mosquito fish, both of which eat mosquito larvae.

Finally, it's worth mentioning that ponds require more maintenance than other water features. In the words of landscape architect Craig Bergmann, "You need to be willing to spend extra time on a pond. They're wonderful to have, but lots of work."

GARDEN DESIGNER
TARA DILLARD ON

Ponds

A pond should be self-contained, with no outside water sources running into it, and it should be good-sized. The most common mistake I see is ponds that are too small. Mosquitoes can be a problem, but adding goldfish takes care of that, and ponds with moving water won't have mosquitoes. Be wary of creating a ledge inside your pond, as this is a great spot for raccoons to stand while catching your fish. Oak leaves make the water acidic, and weeping-willow leaves contain the same ingredient as aspirin; both should be kept out of your pond. A metal heron statue will help keep the real thing away, something your fish will appreciate."

RIGHT Centered with a carved stone fountain, this brick-lined pond is deep enough for a variety of water plants to thrive.

OPPOSITE PAGE, TOP Two small rigid-liner ponds were installed next to one another to create a larger pond that looks like a single unit.

OPPOSITE PAGE, BOTTOM In a sophisticated pairing of stone and water, this lovely pool boasts natural-rock edging, a sloping entry of submerged flagstone, poolside sculptural boulders, and a vanishing edge.

Pond Life

If you plan to have fish and plants in your pond, place it where it will get at least 6 hours of sunlight per day. To protect fish from predators, design your pond so that its sides drop at least 2½ feet straight down, or place pieces of wide drainpipe on the bottom so the fish can hide there. If you want to overwinter goldfish where temperatures get very low, part of the pond should be at least 2 feet deep. Koi need an area that's 3 feet deep.

Check with your local nursery about which water plants are best suited to your area, or purchase one of the collections of pond plants offered by suppliers over the Internet. These are grouped based on climate and pond size, and they typically include all the plants you'll need for a well-balanced pond. Some plants are used mostly for oxygenating the water, particularly important if fish are making a home there; these often float on or just beneath the water's surface. Other pond plants, including the popular lotus and water lily, are grown in submerged pots. Plants that float on the pond's surface, like water hyacinth and water lettuce, can multiply rapidly. This is not a serious problem in your own pond (you can scoop out the excess), but be sure they don't wind up in local wild waterways.

Water Bowls

One of the simplest yet most effective water features you can add to your garden is a stone bowl kept filled to the brim. The water's surface acts as a mirror, bringing a bit of sky down to ground level. Some boulders have natural depressions that will hold water if the stone is oriented correctly, and these are especially serene looking. Place a water bowl next to a bench or at the top of steps—anywhere you want to encourage people to pause for a moment. Be sure to refresh the water frequently to discourage mosquitoes.

Serene and stable, this moss-encrusted stone bowl looks like it might have been in this spot for ages, reflecting passing clouds and starry skies.

Water Features Everywhere

THIS PAGE Surrounded by white and red roses, the limestone steps are attractive whether the fountain is on or off. A whimsical stone ball is poised halfway up, and a rough, broad edging stone marks the boundary between path and pond.

OPPOSITE PAGE, TOP As soon as you enter this courtyard through the wooden front gate, which Colombo designed, you're greeted by the sound of a bubbling stream.

OPPOSITE PAGE, BOTTOM LEFT A lush clump of fountain grass (*Pennisetum* 'Fairy Tails') screens the small collecting pool at the base of this simple but elegant stone fountain.

OPPOSITE PAGE, BOTTOM RIGHT Practically obscured by bellflower, thyme, and grasses, a small bubbling fountain makes its presence known mostly by sound.

W hen landscape designer Scott Colombo purchased the Spanish-style bungalow that once belonged to his grandparents, he completely reimagined the front yard, which originally contained little besides a circular driveway. Here in the mild climate of San Rafael, California, Colombo created a courtyard garden enclosed by a low limestone wall, and filled it with palms, roses, boxwood hedges, espaliered lemons, and an assortment of distinctive water features. Rather than big splashing fountains, which might have overwhelmed the relatively small space, he installed two small bubbling fountains, a gentle dripping cascade of water over limestone steps, and an unobtrusive splashing fountain made from an antique stone column. The combined sound of moving water does an excellent job of masking noise from the nearby street, besides creating a delightfully natural soundscape within the garden walls.

The Elements

- **Boxed-in Stream.** A small rectangular fountain edged with limestone blocks and trimmed box-woods is aligned with the front door and entry gate.

- **Paving.** Close-set tile pavers from France and Tunisia were set in a diamond pattern in the entryway.

- **Walls.** Roughly trimmed blocks of mortared yellow Osage limestone were used to create the walls separating the garden from the street.

- **Water Steps.** The main water feature is a set of limestone steps, where water splashes repeatedly on its way to a small collecting pool.

- **Column Fountain.** An antique stone column was fitted with a simple pipe to form an elegant recirculating fountain.

- **Small Bubbling Fountain.** Tucked into a corner of the garden is a fourth water feature, an unassuming little fountain that bubbles up at ground level.

- **Flagstones.** Widely spaced flagstones accommodate fragrant thyme and chamomile in their generous seams.

- **Plants.** Billowing shrub roses and soft-looking grasses help offset the hard edges of the stonescaping.

Chapter 7

Entryways, Side Yards, and Driveways

Entryways, side yards, and driveways all offer unique possibilities for adding stone to your landscape. The front entry is likely one of the most heavily traveled and highly visible parts of your property—good reasons for showcasing it with durable, attractive stonework. Side yards are often neglected, treated as passageways rather than garden areas that might be developed more fully. And driveways are more utilitarian still; they are often ignored as design elements, despite their prominence and size. In this chapter, you'll see a host of different ways that stone can enhance these varied spaces.

Entryways

The main entrance to your home is a key focal point of your landscape. It makes a lasting first impression on visitors and has a small, subtle effect on you and your family each time you pass through it. Since it's also likely to be an area of heavy use, the entryway is a great place to take advantage of the beauty and strength of stone.

A stone entryway looks appropriate with a variety of house styles, from traditional to contemporary, and it combines well with most building materials. Landscape architect Craig

Bergmann says: "I like using stone for the entry of a brick house, as it provides relief from all the patterning of small units that brick can create. Typically we would use a rectilinear cut stone for fewer joints and a cleaner, simpler appearance, but irregular cobbles or split granite boulders can look great with some houses." A stucco home might lend itself to an entryway of flagstones, set closely for the landing at the front door and stacked for the steps leading up to it. Brick and concrete pavers also make a pleasing contrast to the textured surface of stucco.

LEFT A graciously proportioned stone stairway includes two small terraces to slow the ascent. Twin pillars and a neatly edged cobblestone driveway enhance the formality of the entry.

TOP RIGHT A fanciful blue metal gate signals entry into a courtyard, where the wide joints of a flagstone path accommodate a carpeting ground cover. Multicolored flagstones contrast with the single hue of the walls.

RIGHT Cut bluestone makes an elegant facing for these entry steps.

If your home has an uninspiring concrete pad outside the front door, increase the curb appeal by dressing it up with stain or by covering it with flagstones set in mortar. Another option is replacing the pad with a small stone patio, perhaps incorporating a low wall that gives a feeling of enclosure and arrival to the space. You might even consider adding two large boulders or columnar stones that act as sentinels on either side of the entry. The choices are many, but make sure that your entryway is well lit and easily navigated.

TOP LEFT Twin rows of stepping-stones lead to an entry patio floored with the same stones set close. The sculpture invites closer inspection, drawing you toward the entry, while the patio's edging of cobblestones set in dark mortar calls attention to the change in elevation.

MIDDLE LEFT A small raised pond adds interest to the entry of a traditional brick home. The path surrounding the pond tempts you to stroll around it—and perhaps perch on the wide capstone or relax in the nearby chair—before proceeding to the front door.

BOTTOM LEFT For dramatic contrast with the crisp angles of this contemporary home, a sinuous line of pebbles was set into a concrete walk stained to match them.

RIGHT Sometimes a "straight shot" walkway from the street to the door makes sense, especially when it leads the eye to both the house and the dramatic view beyond.

Entry Paths and Steps

The transition from public to private space actually begins at the street or the edge of the driveway, so be sure the path and steps used to reach the front door reflect thoughtful consideration. For a unifying look, make the path and steps of the same material, and carry that surface right up to the front door.

A formal, symmetrical house squarely facing the street might look best with an extra-wide path leading straight from the

sidewalk to generously proportioned steps up to the front door. Brick or cut-stone pavers would work well for this design. For more casual architectural styles, such as cottage or ranch, a gently curving path is a good choice, perhaps one that leads visitors around a flower bed or cherished tree, or to a small bench next to a water feature. Flagstone pavers would work well for this, but brick could be charming too. For a contemporary home, large concrete pads can be striking as an entry path. Concrete pavers and smooth cut stone also work well.

Again, be sure that the route from the street, sidewalk, or driveway is easy to navigate, with no slippery spots or rough edges that might trip up visitors. If you use fieldstones or flagstones, place the largest pieces at the beginning and end of the path.

Side Yards

This side yard has just enough room for a concrete patio, a dining table, and a curving path leading to the backyard.

Side yards, even more so than driveways, are probably the most overlooked areas in home landscapes. Typically narrow and shady passages leading from the front yard to the back, they can be a design challenge. A simple solution that works in almost any narrow, shady side yard is a stepping-stone path winding between low-maintenance, shade-loving plants like ferns, hostas, hellebores, boxwood, and oakleaf hydrangea, perhaps interspersed with a few small boulders. If there's room, consider adding a few small understory trees like Japanese maple, stewartia, or flowering dogwood. Vines are also a good choice for small spaces like these, whether trained onto a fence or climbing a couple of arching trellises at either end of the space.

In a slightly larger side yard, you can pave part or all of it with gravel, flagstones, or cut stones, and use it in a more utilitarian way. A small garden shed for tools and supplies might fit nicely, as could a compost bin or potting bench.

TOP LEFT A bit of whimsy draws you into this side yard—a semicircular arrangement of concrete pavers that mirrors the curve of the wooden arch. Note the tidy edging of real brick.

TOP RIGHT Irregular fieldstone steps harmonize nicely with a rustic fence and exuberant planting scheme. The chair in the distance as well as the white flowers near it draw the eye into the space.

BOTTOM A spectacularly oversized planter marks the transition from front yard to side yard, where a curving path leads the eye and invites exploration. Unfussy concrete and gravel make perfect sense for the paths.

LEFT Concrete pavers and spheres transform this narrow strip into an artistic, fun space. A compact barberry (*Berberis* x *irwinii*) lines the left side of the path, and horsetail (*Equisetum hymenale*) stands tall and straight on the right. The rain chain adds a finishing touch.

RIGHT Like a slice of tropical jungle, this narrow side yard includes irregular moss-covered stone pavers, colorful bromeliads, tree ferns, cycads, and an enticing statue as the focal point.

A side yard can also be just the spot for a little hidden retreat outfitted with a comfortable chair and small table snuggled into a corner next to a fountain, a hammock swaying above fragrant ground covers, or a bench placed along a wall opposite a flowering vine trained against a fence.

Practical matters to keep in mind include allowing space and access for utility meters, which are often located in side yards. Also keep in mind the view from the house, as windows are likely to afford a close-up view of the landscaping. It's smart as well to make sure you leave enough room in your side-yard design for a wheelbarrow to pass through easily.

LEFT An orderly composition of stacked flagstones, chosen to match the color of the brick driveway, leads to a gated side yard. Vines, crevice plants, and a couple of casually elegant planters enliven the scene.

RIGHT In this small side yard, shade-loving hellebores, ferns, and lily turf *(Liriope gigantea)* thrive among fieldstones. A prefabricated bamboo fence hides the neighbor's trash cans.

A Side-Yard Stonescape

The late-afternoon sun spotlights a lovely stone bench with millstone back. Visitors are sure to pause here before entering the backyard.

RIGHT Unassuming yet comfortable wooden furniture keeps the focus on the stonework.

FAR RIGHT Intersecting the side-yard path is a similar path of mortared flagstone. Large containers visually break up the space.

A shady side-yard garden in Atlanta, Georgia, was just a way to get from the front of the house to the backyard. But with the installation of a stone path and custom-built bench, it became a favorite part of the garden. As garden designer Tara Dillard points out, "The site was chosen as a shady destination just right for reading or alfresco dining, and a pair of old millstones were selected as focal points." Rugged types of stone were selected to match the style of the older home, and a path and custom-built bench were installed. A millstone incorporated into the path draws the eye and seems to enlarge the small area, and a second one contributes to a unique bench. A few wooden folding chairs and tables have made their way into the space, where the homeowner often entertains family and friends.

The Elements

- **Stone Path.** A path of close-set, mortared flagstone, which includes a millstone, makes a stable path that is easy to keep clean.

- **Edging.** Matching cobbles stand on edge to separate path from planting beds.

- **Stone Bench.** A custom fieldstone bench with a millstone back is perfectly proportioned for maximum comfort, and it's just the right height to accommodate a dining table.

- **Wooden Chairs and Table.** Lightweight furniture can be moved about the space, depending on the occasion.

- **Containers.** Matching terra-cotta pots with a raised design add an elegant touch to the rustic side yard.

- **Trellis.** An open-form metal trellis that looks great with or without foliage marks the entrance to an intersecting path.

- **Trees.** Small deciduous trees provide shade in the hot days of summer. In winter, their bare branches allow more light into the space.

Driveways

LEFT Sand-colored concrete pavers are the perfect choice for this driveway, bounded by white stucco walls and a dramatic black garage door. A thoughtful planting scheme provides soft texture and pleasing color alongside the drive.

RIGHT This charming patchwork was made from broken pieces of the former concrete driveway, interspersed with granite blocks and edged with granite boulders.

BELOW RIGHT Contrasting concrete pavers provide visual relief in an expansive concrete driveway and parking area. Large spaces like this call for bold patterns.

Even though they're usually large and highly visible features of a property, driveways are often overlooked as a potential area for improving the look of a home. They're treated as an unfortunate necessity, sometimes too narrow or small, and too often made of stained, cracked cement or asphalt installed when the house was built and never considered again.

There are any number of ways to dress up your driveway. You might have the existing concrete stained or top-coated in a color or finish that complements your home. Or, you might widen a narrow drive by adding a walkway of a contrasting material like brick or cut stone along one or both sides. To add interest, have a center strip cut from your driveway and fill it with a contrasting material, such as small stones or even low-growing ground covers, to break up the monotony.

If you'd rather replace your old driveway altogether, you have even more options. A new concrete drive is perhaps the simplest alternative, and decorative effects like seeded aggregate, staining, or stamping and tooling can give it a custom look. Cobblestones are a favored material, being highly durable and exceedingly handsome. They also create a somewhat permeable surface, allowing water to seep down into the soil rather than running off into the street. Bricks and concrete pavers are other semi-permeable choices, and they can be laid in attractive patterns that give visual relief to the large expanse. Gravel is another good material for a driveway, especially with an attractive stone edging to keep it in place. Garden designer Tara Dillard says: "Coming home to the sound of tires on gravel or crossing stones is a joy to the soul. A gravel driveway edged with cobblestones is classic, but don't use gravel larger than 1 to 1½ inches, or it will make your driveway look commercial." When it comes to adding stone elements along the edge of a driveway, landscape architect Craig Bergmann makes these points: "If we are using large stones to mark the edge of a driveway, we make sure they are set back at least 12 inches from the pavement edge so vehicles are less likely to hit them. In cold climates, they must be able to withstand the impact of a snowplow, and they need to be below or well above the average height of a car bumper—for example, 8 inches or shorter or 24 inches or greater."

TOP This asphalt driveway was decorated with whimsical brick inlays that are in perfect harmony with the style of the house.

ABOVE Wide concrete edgings and matching gateposts give contemporary appeal to this classic brick driveway. A massive boulder stands guard among the greenery.

RIGHT Pretty enough to use as a sitting area, this driveway was given a makeover that included staining and scoring the concrete and adding a central strip of loose river stones.

Getting It Done

Throughout this book, we've looked at a variety of ways to use stone and stone-like materials in the landscape, from creating simple flagstone paths and small getaways to installing more involved projects like stone fountains and patios that incorporate outdoor kitchens. In this chapter, we'll lay out some of the steps you can take to get your projects moving plus things to keep in mind as you develop your plan, like drainage, lighting, and irrigation. We'll also suggest ways you can keep your patio and stonescaping projects eco-friendly, and offer some pointers on working with professionals.

Creating a Design

Once you've identified the projects you'd like to do, it's time to start the planning process. Even if you'll be hiring someone to help out or to do the entire job, you'll want to take some preliminary steps toward organizing the tasks and understanding what's involved.

Drawing a Plan

For a project that calls for reorganizing the space, such as adding a patio, a path, or a new set of raised beds, it's a good idea to map out your property. Even if you've lived with a landscape for many years, drawing a plan of the space is a great way to re-evaluate its potential and

see it as a designer would. You may save time if you can locate a deed map or architectural plan that gives the dimensions of your property. Or measure the property yourself, with a 50- or 100-foot tape measure and a helper. Start with a rough sketch of the property's outline, then measure all boundaries and

determine north, and mark it on your plan. This will help you identify patterns of sun and shade that change with the time of day and seasons.

Once you've taken the measurements, you're ready to draw a base plan to scale, essentially a bird's-eye view of your property. You can draw the plan on graph paper or, if you prefer, choose a landscape-design software package to lay out your plan digitally. Choose a scale that allows you to fit the entire plan on a single sheet (for instance, making each square equal to 2 feet). Once you've drawn your base plan, you can lay tracing paper over it to try out different designs, or make several copies of the plan and sketch your ideas directly on them. Garden designer Tara Dillard suggests the following: "Create an inspiration folder of pictures of gardens, plants, focal points, and furnishings you like. Spread these out on a table and begin trying out your ideas on paper. Not all of your ideas will pass the drawing test, but it's a valuable learning process."

When you have a rough idea of where you want your new landscape features, go outside and mock up the design. Use flour or limestone powder to sketch out free-form shapes, and wooden stakes and string for linear elements. Test out locations for a seating area with a lawn chair, and be sure to try it at various times of day. Tara Dillard notes: "This is a funny progression of moving around old chairs, things from the garage, and plastic flags to mark the location of stones and plants. Adjust this 'rough draft' over a period of several days to be sure your project is laid out just the way you want it."

dimensions of the lot, as well as the outlines of your house and other structures. Make a notation of any doors and windows, including the height of lower-story windows. Mark the position of hose bibs, downspouts, sidewalks, gates, and all trees, shrubs, and garden beds you wish to keep. Use a compass to

Keeping It Legal

If you plan to do any major construction, check local zoning and landscape construction laws, such as those concerning setback requirements and safety codes for pools and spas. Your property deed will give you the exact location of property lines, easements, and rights of way, as well as restrictions on building projects and tree removal. Contact your water and utility companies with any questions about water and power lines or underground cabling.

OPPOSITE PAGE You may not have this sort of overhead view of your garden space, but you can draw a plan to scale to approximate it. Your plan will give you a clear idea of how the different elements relate to one another.

ABOVE Basic drafting tools like a ruler, compass, and bendable curved-line tool make it easy to draw up your base plan on graph paper.

Planning for Drainage

Anytime you pave an area or install a large landscape feature such as a wall or pond, the natural drainage is affected. Water runs off or around these structures and can pool at their edges. A gravel patio laid on a bed of sand is permeable enough that it won't impede drainage much, and neither will a path of small stepping-stones.

But for larger installations involving less permeable materials, you'll need to consider ways to handle the runoff.

On a flat site, a patio is often constructed so that a drain sits at its lowest point (often in the center) and carries the water away through a buried pipe. Otherwise, for paved areas like patios or driveways, it's a good idea

to grade the area slightly, with a pitch of at least 1 inch for every 8 feet to allow the water to drain quickly away. At the downhill edge of the patio, you'll need a drainage system to prevent puddles. The most basic option is a gravel-filled trench, dug about 12 inches deep (deeper where soil freezes) and about as wide. For even better drainage, bury a perforated drainpipe near the bottom of the trench with its holes pointed downward, sloping the pipe so that it carries water away from the area. If you don't like the look of gravel, you can dig the trench a little deeper and fill it with gravel topped by a layer of landscape fabric and about 4 inches of soil; then plant turf or ground cover.

You can also use a drainpipe to divert water to a dry creekbed or a dry well, which is simply a large hole filled with rounded gravel where water slowly percolates into the surrounding soil. Or lead the pipe to a planting area downhill that can handle the extra water. In areas with frequent or heavy rains, consider creating a rain garden and diverting the water there. To create a rain garden, outline an area at least 10 feet long and wide and excavate to a depth of about 8 inches, using the dug soil to create a raised area around the edges of a flat site or on the downhill side of a sloping site. Mix in a generous amount of compost, and plant shrubs or perennials that can withstand periodic flooding. (Check with your local nursery for plant selections.)

Planning for Irrigation

Before you get started installing a patio, raised bed, or other stone feature, give some thought to how it might affect your existing irrigation system or how you might incorporate irrigation into the new project. Be sure you know the location of any buried irrigation lines to avoid cutting through them when excavating. If you're adding a vertical feature like a wall or an upright stone sculpture, take note of how it may block the spray of water from sprinklers. Decorative stone elements may benefit from being rinsed off regularly, but be sure patios, paths, and steps are not being sprayed when people are likely to be using them.

If you're building a patio and plan to furnish it with containers, consider including PVC lines beneath it, with T-connectors providing openings where irrigation lines can emerge near the pots. If you're building a new raised bed, plan for any buried irrigation lines to run alongside the walls, not through the middle of the bed. Leave a small hole in the wall where you can run in the main line unobtrusively and connect it to aboveground emitters. Buried irrigation lines can also be located beneath paths, where you're less likely to be digging. If a raised sprinkler head is too prominent from a particular viewpoint, hide it behind a stone, but be sure the spray is not impeded. A group of boulders can attractively shield from view a hose bib or in-ground electrical box.

TOP LEFT Pop-up sprinklers keep this planting bed well irrigated and the decorative boulder rinsed clean.

ABOVE Situated at the bottom of a fairly steep slope, this dining area would be in danger of flooding if less permeable paving had been used. A gravel path and open-jointed patio of cut stones ensure that the water percolates down into the soil.

Low-voltage lights cast a soft glow on this garden path, while standard fixtures provide a more dramatic effect on the home's columns. On the porch, overhead fixtures provide the same level of light that you might expect indoors.

Planning for Lighting

Lighting provides safety, security, and decoration to the landscape. If you're adding a patio or water element, you'll definitely want to include lighting so that the space can be used safely at night. Entryways and driveways are obvious spots for lighting, but a subtly lit fountain, pathway, or stone stairway adds nighttime interest and ambience to the garden, whether you're enjoying it outdoors or observing it from inside. When it comes to outdoor lighting, several soft lights are better than a single bright one. Place fixtures low (such as knee-high along a walkway) or high (such as in a tree or along an eave). Avoid glaring lights at eye level.

For a small patio or an intimate getaway, the soft glow of candles or lanterns may provide all the illumination you need. Solar lights are another option. They require no power other than that stored from the sun, but after a cloudy day, they won't be charged enough to light up. Electric-light choices include

standard 120-volt systems, with buried cable and substantial metallic fixtures, and low-voltage systems, which step down household current to 12 volts and use thin, flexible cables to run power to the fixtures. Low-voltage systems are safer, more energy efficient, and easier to install. Although most lighting fixtures are made of metal or plastic, you can find decorative ones fashioned from stone, concrete, porcelain, or wood.

LANDSCAPE ARCHITECT
CRAIG BERGMANN ON

Garden Lighting

Do-it-yourself landscape lighting can be tricky. Inexpensive lighting systems are generally short-lived and require lots of maintenance, and many decorative fixtures call too much attention to themselves and can date a landscape. Lighting consultants do a great job of showcasing the light itself, rather than the fixtures. We usually recommend a system of durable fixtures designed by a consultant and installed by experienced professionals, even if the clients have to phase in the installation over a few years due to budget restrictions."

Keeping It Green

Every little bit helps. These homeowners reduced the size of their lawn with a flagstone pathway planted with woolly thyme and other unthirsty ground covers. This design conserves water, reduces the need for fertilizer and herbicides, and means less mowing.

We've mentioned a few ways to make various landscape projects more environmentally friendly. Here's a recap, along with a few other suggestions for conserving resources and protecting the environment.

- Use stone from the nearest source. If you have stones on your property, use them. Otherwise, choose stones collected or quarried locally to cut down on fuel used for transport.

- Once in place, most stonework requires no maintenance or resources to stay looking great year-round.

- Reduce the size of your resource-gobbling lawn by adding a patio or even just a pathway along one side.

- Opt for low-voltage or solar-powered lighting and fountains.

- Choose natural gas for your outdoor fireplace, fire pit, or grill. It burns more cleanly than wood.

- To reduce wasteful runoff, choose permeable paving materials such as an open-cell driveway paving system or a stepping-stone path set in gravel.

- Set lights or running fountains on timers; for lights, consider daylight-sensitive photocells or motion-sensor fixtures.

- Use a broom to clean your patio, driveway, or path, rather than a jet of water from the hose.

- Be sure to grade for on-site drainage, and consider adding a French drain, dry creekbed, rain garden, or series of terraces to prevent runoff.

- Reuse old bricks, broken concrete, and other hardscape materials whenever possible.

- Install a cover for your swimming pool. This will reduce the energy needed for heating, cut down on evaporation, and minimize the amount of chemicals needed.

TOP A green driveway made of 1-foot-square pavers interplanted with grass reduces runoff and harmonizes beautifully with this contemporary design.

MIDDLE Who needs a lawn anyway? This backyard has been transformed into a spacious gravel patio surrounded by raised beds made from local stone.

BOTTOM Not every garden can be as drought tolerant as this one, but an arrangement of boulders can fit into many landscape styles. Stone is the ultimate low-maintenance garden element.

Working with Professionals

Professional designers keep up with current trends in hardscaping and plant materials, like this trendy variegated agave featured in a rusty, industrial-chic planter.

RIGHT Huge boulders—including one that incorporates a subtle fountain—edge this expansive flagstone patio decorated with a river of inset pebbles. A project like this calls for professional help.

Some of the simpler features we've seen in this book, such as a stepping-stone path, a low raised bed, or even a small recirculating fountain, can be accomplished by a do-it-yourselfer in a weekend or two. Larger projects, like pools, large patios, and walls, will almost certainly require the assistance of a landscape professional.

LANDSCAPE ARCHITECTS are licensed to design exterior structures, solve complicated drainage and elevation problems, and give advice on where to place service lines, entries, driveways, and parking areas.

LANDSCAPE DESIGNERS OR GARDEN DESIGNERS may be self-taught or may have the same academic credentials as a landscape architect, but do not have a state license. They are more likely to work on smaller, strictly residential projects.

LICENSED LANDSCAPE CONTRACTORS are trained in methods of earthmoving, construction, and planting. They may subcontract specialty jobs like electrical work, water feature installation, or wall building.

STONEMASONS AND BRICKLAYERS are artisans trained in the special skills needed to build with stone and brick.

HORTICULTURISTS specialize in the selection and care of garden plants.

Landscape architect Craig Bergmann has this advice: "Collect a file of ideas before your interview with a professional, and make sure you see finished projects so that you can evaluate their quality. If you're planning on doing a project yourself, talk to professionals before investing too much money to make sure you understand what's involved."

Scott Colombo, landscape designer, concurs: "Collect photos of gardens or elements you like, to assist your designer in understanding what you are trying to achieve. Always ask to see samples of their work to understand their abilities and design sense more fully. If your project involves significant grade changes, serious drainage issues, or more complicated issues, always consult a professional, as it will save you a lot of time, money, and frustration in the long run."

In the words of garden designer Tara Dillard: "Landscaping is done on a template, so you don't have to re-create the wheel. Make a landscape plan and divide it into phases, some of which you can do yourself and some for which you'll need to hire an expert."

Resource Guide

The following pages list organizations, manufacturers, and retailers that you might find helpful in creating your new patio or stonescape, with an emphasis on companies dedicated to environmentally responsible manufacturing processes and products. To find a local source for stone, check online sources listed here for local dealers or look in the Yellow Pages under these headings: Stone-Natural, Stone-Landscaping, Quarries, Rock, Building Materials, Landscape Equipment and Supplies.

Organizations and Associations

American Society of Landscape Architects
www.asla.org
202-898-2444, 888-999-2752

Association of Professional Landscape Designers
www.apld.com
717-238-9780

Building Materials Reuse Association
www.buildingreuse.org
800-990-2672

The Association of Pool and Spa Professionals
www.apsp.org
703-838-0083

North American Rock Garden Society
www.nargs.org

Stonescaping Products

Allan Block Corporation
www.allanblock.com
952-835-5309
Stackable block for retaining walls and vertical walls

Butterfield Color
www.butterfieldcolor.com
800-282-3388
Concrete colorant, stains, stamps

Concrete Art
www.concreteart.net
800-500-9445
Decorative scoring and staining system

Coverall Stone Inc.
www.coverallstone.com
206-937-5200
Natural stone columns, tiles, pebbles, fountains, benches

Cultured Stone
www.culturedstone.com
Manufactured stone

D. A. Spencer Natural Stone Water Sculptures, Inc.
www.naturalstonewater
sculptures.com
585-924-7542
Hand-carved stone sculptures

EP Henry Corporation
www.ephenry.com
Concrete pavers, blocks, veneers

The Garden of Glass
www.thegardenofglass.com
800-571-7611
Glass aggregate

Goshen Stone Co., Inc.
www.goshenstone.com
413-268-7171
Natural stone

The Home Depot
www.homedepot.com
Building and landscaping materials, patio furnishings

Lowe's Home Improvement
www.lowes.com
Building and landscaping materials, patio furnishings

Lyngso Garden Materials, Inc.
www.lyngsogarden.com
650-364-1730
Natural stone

L & W Stone Corporation
www.lwstonecorp.com
800-346-9739
Natural stone pavers, boulders, veneer

Paver Search
www.paversearch.com
Paver products and resources

Robinson Brick
www.robinsonbrick.com
800-477-9002
Brick and thin true-stone veneer

StoneDeck West, Inc.
www.stonedeckwest.com
877-686-4759
Natural stone decking systems

Sure-loc Edging
www.surelocedging.com
800-787-3562
Aluminum and steel landscape and paver edging

The Stone Yard
www.stoneyard.com
800-231-2200
Natural building and landscaping stone for walls and patios

Watsontown Brick Co.
www.watsontownbrick.com
800-538-2040

Mail-Order Sources for Rock-Garden Plants

Evermay Nursery
www.evermaynursery.com
207-827-0522

Mt. Tahoma Nursery
www.backyardgardener.com/mttahoma
253-847-9827

Siskiyou Rare Plant Nursery
www.srpn.net
541-535-7103

Trennoll Nursery
PO Box 125
Trenton, OH 45067-1614
513-988-6121

Wild Ginger Farm
www.wildgingerfarm.com
503-632-2338

Patio Furniture and Accessories

All-Safe Pool Safety Barriers
www.allsafepool.com
800-786-8110
Pool fences, safety net pool covers

Allsop Home Garden
www.allsopgarden.com
866-425-5767
Solar lanterns and garden art

The Blue Rooster Company
www.theblauerooster.com
800-303-4312
Chimeneas

Cal Spas
www.calspas.com
800-225-7727
Prefab barbecues, fire pits, fireplaces

Patiolife.com
www.patiolife.com
877-897-2846
Outdoor patio furniture

Iron Age Designs
www.ironagegrates.com
206-276-0925
Drain and tree grates and architectural castings

Restoration Hardware
www.restorationhardware.com
800-910-9836
Outdoor furniture and umbrellas

Smith & Hawken
www.smithandhawken.com
800-940-1170
Outdoor rugs, furniture, accessories

Sunbrella
www.sunbrella.com
Outdoor fabric

Whit McLeod
www.whitmcleod.com
707-822-7307
Outdoor furniture made from reclaimed lumber

Outdoor Kitchens

Barbeques Galore
www.bbqgalore.com
800-752-3085
Barbecues and accessories

Fogazzo Wood Fired Ovens and BBQs
www.fogazzo.com
866-364-2996

Marvel Scientific
www.marvelscientific.com
800-962-2521
Outdoor refrigerators

Syndecrete
www.syndecrete.com
Concrete slab countertops

Vetrazzo
www.vetrazzo.com
510-234-5550
Recycled glass countertops

Weber-Stephen Products Co.
www.weber.com
800-446-1071
Outdoor appliances and accessories

Credits

Photography

Courtesy of Mark Armstrong/Iron Age Designs: 210; Karen Aitken: 19 top right, 20–23 all, 26, 33 top, 35 top right, 39 bottom, 47 bottom left, 48 top, 62, 75 bottom left, 118 bottom left, 122, 143 bottom; Botanica/Jupiter Images: 132, 149 top right, 160, 163 bottom; Paul Bousquet: 199 left; Marion Brenner: 25 top right, 31 right, 81 top right, 103 middle right, 103 bottom right, 129 middle, 137 bottom right, 153 top right, 157 bottom right, 164 middle left, 183 top, 199 right; Rob D. Brodman: 3 left, 3 right, 25 bottom right, 28, 45, 47 right, 53 top, 53 bottom, 61, 79 top right, 85 bottom middle, 101 bottom right, 107 top right, 139, 147, 149 bottom right, 175 bottom right, 176 left, 196, 198 left, 207, 208, 211 right, 213 right, 215 top; Judith Bromley: 204 top; Linda Oyama Bryan: 88–89 all, 220; Karen Bussolini: 103 top, 103 bottom middle; Van Chaplin/SPC: 2 right, 113, 159 bottom right; Peter Christiansen: 41 2nd from top; Claire Curran: 102; Andrew Drake: 127 bottom right; Miki Duisterhof/Botanica/Jupiter Images: 17; Roger Foley: 12 bottom left, 19 bottom right, 30 right, 40 top right, 40 middle right, 42 top right, 47 top left, 49, 54 left, 60 all, 63 top right, 68, 76 top right, 76 bottom right, 80 top, 81 top middle, 85 top right, 86 left, 91, 96 bottom right, 106, 110 all, 111 bottom, 114, 119, 123 top right, 123 bottom middle, 129 top right, 134, 135 bottom left, 140, 141, 155 top, 169, 170, 171 bottom, 174, 184, 185 right, 187 bottom,

192, 194 top left, 194 middle left, 197 top right, 212; Fyletto/bigstockphotos.com: 99 right; Frank Gaglione: 41 bottom middle, 41 3rd from top right, 43 top, 43 top right, 43 bottom left; David Goldberg/Susan Roth & Co.: 99 left; Steven Gunther: 55, 66, 73 bottom, 77, 81 bottom, 92, 124, 171 top right, 172, 179 right, 181 top, 183 bottom, 195, 215 bottom, 216; Jamie Hadley: 71 bottom right; Marcus Harpur: 98 right; Philip Harvey: 41 top, 41 bottom right, 121 bottom right; Saxon Holt: 2 left, 7, 8, 14, 27, 29 all, 50, 54 right, 57 top, 74, 76 bottom left, 83 middle right, 96 bottom left, 108, 156, 159 top right, 205, 215 middle; D. A. Horchner/Design Workshop: 116, 125 top right; istockphoto.com: 138 bottom left; JBT/Photolibrary.com: 165; Jon Jensen: 51 left; Michael Jensen: 80 bottom; Andrea Jones/Garden Exposures: 69 bottom; Judy White/GardenPhotos.com: 35 bottom right, 143 top; Jupiter Images: 173 top left; Caroline Kopp: 155 bottom, 173 bottom right; N. D. Koster: back flap; Chuck Kuhn: 43 middle; Jason Liske: 36–37 all, 84, 87 left, 104, 105, 115 bottom, 117 top, 125 bottom right, 175 bottom left, 177, 197 bottom, 204 bottom; Janet Loughrey: 83 top right, 163 top, 163 middle; Maggie MacLaren: 52; Allan Mandell: 40 top left, 42 top left, 101 top right, 131 bottom right, 164 bottom left; Charles Mann: 133 bottom left, 133 bottom right, 173 bottom left; Jim McCausland: 32, 95 bottom left, 135

top right; courtesy of Mutual Materials: 33 middle, 33 bottom; Jerry Pavia: 16, 96 top, 126, 127 top, 131 top right, 158 top right, 164 top left; Jerry Pavia/Photolibrary.com: 161 top left, 162; Linda Lamb Peters: 58 bottom left, 76 top left, 82, 180 bottom right; Norm Plate: 72 bottom right, 118 top left, 121 top right, 125 middle left, 153 top middle, 178, 217; Norman A. Plate: 152 top right, 203 top; Ken Rice/Corner House Stock Photo: 145 top; Lisa Romerein: 24; Susan A. Roth: 128; JS Sira/Photolibrary.com: 161 top right, 161 bottom; courtesy of D.A. Spencer Sculptures Inc.: 181 bottom; courtesy of Smith & Hawken: 72 bottom left; Tim Street-Porter/Beateworks/Corbis: 35 top left; Thomas J. Story: 3 middle, 10, 30 left, 34, 38, 39 top left, 46, 51 top right, 56, 59, 63 bottom right, 64–65 all, 67 right, 67 bottom right, 71 bottom left, 72 top right, 73 top left, 73 top right, 75 right, 79 bottom right , 85 bottom right, 86 right, 87 right, 93 top left, 95 top, 97, 100 bottom right, 117 bottom, 120, 136, 142, 144, 153 bottom right, 180 top, 180 bottom left, 185 top left, 185 bottom left, 187 top, 191, 193 top, 193 bottom, 194 bottom left, 198 right, 202, 214; Dan Stultz: 209; Joel Tressler: 31 left, 70, 95 bottom right, 101 bottom middle, 200–201 all; Jared Vermeil: 158 bottom right; Deidra Walpole: 135 bottom right, 211 left; Rachel Weill/Jupiter Images: 186 bottom; Lee Anne White: 1, 9 top, 9 bottom, 11 top, 11 bottom, 12 top left, 13, 15 all, 18, 39 top right, 39 middle left, 39 middle right, 48 bottom, 51 bottom right, 57 bottom, 58 top left, 63 bottom left, 69 top, 71 top, 75 top left, 78, 83 bottom right, 93 top right, 93 bottom, 94, 98 left, 100 top right, 103 middle left, 103 bottom left, 107 middle right, 107 bottom right, 109 top right, 109 bottom, 111 top, 115 top right, 123 bottom right, 125 top middle, 127 bottom left, 129 bottom right, 133 top left and right, 135 top left, 138 top left, 145 bottom, 149 left, 150, 152 bottom right, 157 bottom left, 158 bottom left, 171 top left, 173 top right, 175 top, 182, 186 top, 197 top left, 203 bottom, 218; Russ Widstrand/Corner House Stock Photo: 42 middle right; Michele Lee Willson: 40 bottom, 41 bottom left, 130, 148, 154, 157 top right, 157 top left, 166–167 all, 188–189 all, 211 left.

Design

1: Four Dimensions Landscape Co.; 7: Shari Bashin-Sullivan; 8: David Feix Design; 9 top right: The Fockele Garden Company; 9 bottom right: Clemens & Associates, Inc.; 10: Richard Ward; 11 top right: Bill Hewett; 11 bottom right: The Fockele Garden Company; 12 top left: Luis Llenza Garden Design; 12 bottom left: Oehme, van Sweden & Associates; 13: Robert Norris; 14: Michael Thilgen; 15 top: The Fockele Garden Company; 15 bottom: Clemens & Associates, Inc.; 18: Robert Norris; 19 top right: Aitken & Associates; 19 bottom right: Michael Blake, Landscape Architect; 20–23: Aitken & Associates; 24: Russ Cletta; 25 top right: Harland Hand; 25 bottom right: Jon Buerk, J. Buerk Landscape/Maintenance; 26: Aitken & Associates; 27: David Yakish; 28: Windsmith Design; 29 top: Michael Derviss, Landscapes Designed; 29 bottom: Richard Wm. Wogisch; 30 left: Bud Stuckey; 30 right: Richard Arentz, Arentz Landscape Architects; 31 right: Steve Fidrych; 32: Scott Junge, Rosedale Gardens; 33 top: Aitken & Associates; 34: Michael Manneh and Stefan Offermann; 35 top right: Aitken & Associates; 36–37: Bernard Trainor + Associates; 38: Teri Ravel Kane; 39 top left: Shirley Alexandra Watts, 39 middle left: Luis Llenza Garden Design; 39 top right: Jeni Webber; 39 middle right: Clemens & Associates, Inc.; 39 bottom: Aitken & Associates; 40 top left: Jeff Bale; 40 top right: Arentz Landscape Architects; 40 middle right: Dean Riddle; 42 top left: Will Goodman and Michael Schultz; 42 top right: Arentz Landscape Architects; 45: Roberta Walker Landscape Design; 46: Teri Ravel; 47 top left: Scott Brinitzer Design Associates; 47 bottom left: Aitken & Associates; 47 right: Cathy Drees, Accent Gardens; 48 top: Aitken & Associates; 48 bottom: Richard McPherson, Landscape Architects; 49: Raymond Jungles Inc.; 50: Harry North and Jeff Sargent, Creative Environments; 51 left: Landscape contractor: Dean DeSantis, DeSantis Landscapes; Timber-frame construction: Jim DeSantis, Silver Creek Timber Works; 51 top right: Santa Fe Permaculture; 51 bottom right: Hillary Curtis, David Thorne Landscape Architects; 52: Julian Durant, the Hendrikus Group; 53 top: Jon Buerk, J. Buerk Landscape/Maintenance;

53 bottom: Michael Glassman & Associates; 54 left: Scott Brinitzer Design Associates; 54 right: Van Atta Associates; 55: Nancy Goslee Power & Associates; 56: Paul Harris, Imagine Sonoma; 57 top: Kern Hildebrand; 57 bottom: Jeni Webber; 58 top left: P.O.P.S. Landscaping; 58 bottom left: Matthew and Joan Lane, Proscape Landscaping; 59: Huettl-Thuilot Associates; 60 bottom: Donna Hackman; 61: Terry Mulrooney, Admiral Green Landscaping; 62: Aitken & Associates; 63 top right: Arentz Landscape Architects; 63 bottom left: P.O.P.S. Landscaping; 63 bottom right: Steve Morgan; 64–65: Pamela Dreyfuss, Interior Design; Exteriors Landscape Architecture; 66: Margaret West, Margaret West Designs; 67 top right: Theresa Clark Studio; 67 bottom right: Pool and Landscape Design: Andrea Cochran Landscape Architecture; Poolhouse: E. B. Min, Min/Day; 68: Tom Mannion Landscape Design; 69 top: P.O.P.S. Landscaping; 69 bottom: Topher Delaney; 70: Penny McHenry; 71 top: P.O.P.S. Landscaping; 71 bottom left: Susan Collier Lamont, Lamontscapes; Jay Tripathi and Peter Estournes, Gardenworks; 71 bottom right: John Montgomery, ASLA, Garden Architecture; 72 top right: Firepit design: Perry Becker, Perlman Architects; Landscape design: Michael Dollin, Urban Earth Design; 72 bottom right: Mike and Anette Heacox, Luciole Design, Deco Construction; 73 top left: Bud Stuckey; 73 top right: Rob Pressman, TGP Landscape Architecture; 73 bottom: Nick Williams & Associates; 74: Suzanne Porter; 75 top left: Jeni Webber; 75 bottom left: Aitken & Associates; 75 right: Theresa Clark Studio; 76 top left: Elliot Goliger, Artisans Landscape; 76 top right: Scott Brinitzer Design Associates; 76 bottom left: Allen Landscaping; 76 bottom right: Dean Riddle; 77: Pat Brodie Landscape Design; 78: Jeni Webber; 79 bottom right: Mark Bartos; 80 top: Tom Mannion Landscape Design; 81 top right: Tom Wilhite; 81 top middle: Yunghi Choi; 81 bottom: Theresa Clark Studio; 83 middle right: Van Atta Associates; 83 bottom right: Randi Herman; 84: Bernard Trainor + Associates; 85 top right: William Morrow Landscape Design; 85 bottom middle: Rosemary Wells, Viridian Landscape Architecture;

86 left: William Morrow Landscape Design; 87 left: Bernard Trainor + Associates; 87 right: Mark Bartos; 88–89: Craig Bergmann Landscape Design; 91: Clinton & Associates; 92: Ellen Speert, California Center for Creative Renewal; 93 top left: Eric Teberg Landscape Design Service; 93 top right: Four Dimensions Landscape Co.; 93 bottom: The Fockele Garden Company: 94: Randi Herman; 95 top: Mathew Henning and Heather Anderson, Henning-Anderson; 96 bottom left: Roger Raiche; 96 bottom right: Yunghi Choi; 97: Jim and Paula Umbeck; 98 left: The Fockele Garden Company; 98 right: John Wood; 99 left: Richard Wogisch; 100 top right: Richard McPherson, Landscape Architect; 100 bottom right: Susan Collier Lamont, Lamontscapes; Jay Tripathi and Peter Estournes, Gardenworks; 101 top right: Vanessa Nagel, Milieux Design Studio; 101 bottom right: Cathy Drees, Accent Gardens; 102: Sisters Specialty Gardens; 103 top: Dickson DeMarche Landscape Architects; 103 middle left: Hilary Curtis, David Thorne Landscape Architects; 103 bottom left: David Feix and Mario Trejo; 103 bottom right: Davis Dalbok, Living Green; 104–105: Bernard Trainor + Associates; 106: Oehme, van Sweden & Associates; 107 top right: Shari Bashin-Sullivan and Richard Sullivan; 107 middle right: Clemens & Associates, Inc.; 107 bottom right: Robert Norris; 108: Chris Jacobson; 109 top right: Jeni Webber; 109 bottom: The Fockele Garden Company; 110 top: Barbara Katz; 110 middle: Richard Arentz, Arentz Landscape Architects; 111 top: Jeni Webber; 111 bottom: Scott Brinitzer Design Associates; 114: Scott Brinitzer Design Associates; 115 top right: Clemens & Associates, Inc.; 115 bottom right: Bernard Trainor + Associates; 116: Mark Hershberger, Hershberger Design/Design Workshop; 117 top: Bernard Trainor + Associates; 117 bottom: Topher Delaney; 118 top left: Cyndy Scanlon; 118 bottom left: Aitken & Associates; 119: Maggie Juidycki for Green Themes Inc.; 120: Huettl-Thuilot Associates; 121 bottom right: R. M. Bradshaw & Associates; 122: Aitken & Associates; 123 top right, bottom right: Jeni Webber; 123 bottom middle: Yunghi Choi; 124: Rich Grigsby, The Great Outdoors Landscape Design; 125 top

middle: Jeni Webber; 125 middle left: Carolyn & Doug McCord; 125 bottom right: Bernard Trainor + Associates; 127 bottom left: Clemens & Associates, Inc.; 129 top right: Clinton & Associates; 129 middle: Elizabeth Everall Design; 130: Scott Colombo Designs; 131 bottom right: Jeff Bales; 133 top left: Jeni Webber; 133 top right: Four Dimensions Landscape Co.; 134: Raymond Jungles, Inc.; 135 top left: Jeni Webber; 135 bottom left: David Culp; 136: Santa Fe Permaculture; 137 bottom right: Tom Wilhite; 138 top left: Jeni Webber; 139: Kate Mulligan, Liquidambar Garden Design; 140–141: Donna Hackman; 142: Monika Hellwegen and Azul Cobb, Carlotta from Paradise; 143 bottom: Aitken & Associates; 144: Ahna Pietras-Dominski; 145 bottom: Jeni Webber; 147: Windsmith Design; 148: Tom Wilhite; 149 left: Paul & Robin Cowley; 149 bottom right: Windsmith Design; 150: Simmonds & Associates; 152 top right: Jana Ruzicka; 152 bottom right: The Fockele Garden Company; 153 top middle: Steven Sternke, Magic Gardens; 153 top right: Tom Wilhite; 153 bottom right: Enchanted Plantings; 154: Tom Wilhite; 155 top: Clinton & Associates; 156: Barbara Foster; 157 top left: Scott Colombo Designs; 157 top right: Tom Wilhite; 157 bottom left: The Fockele Garden Company; 158 top right: Margie Grace; 158 bottom left: Richard McPherson, Landscape Architect; 158 bottom right: vermeilDesign; 159 top right: David Gemes; 159 bottom right: Pratt Brown; 163 top: Phyllis Gustafson; 163 middle: Kathy Allen; 164 middle left: Tom Wilhite; 166–167: Tom Wilhite; 169: Tom Mannion Landscape Design; 170: Armstrong-Berger; 171 top left: The Fockele Garden Company; 171 bottom: Tom Mannion Landscape Design; 173 top right: Clemens & Associates; 173 bottom left: Carlotta from Paradise; 174: DCA Landscape Architects; 175 top: The Fockele Garden Company; 175 bottom left: Bernard Trainor + Associates; 175 bottom right: Rosemary Wells, Viridan Landscape Architecture; 176: Cathy Drees, Accent Gardens; 177: Bernard Trainor + Associates; 178: Barbara Simon Landscape Design; Dinsdale Landscape Contractors; 179 right: Jeffrey Gordon Smith; 180 top: Brian Baird, Scenic Scapes; 180 bottom left: Jim & Paula

Umbeck; 180 bottom right: Elliot Goliger, Artisans Landscape; 181 top: Margaret West, Margaret West Design; 181 bottom: D. A. Spencer Sculptures Inc.; 182: Richard McPherson, Landscape Architect; 183 top: Roger Warner Designs; 184: Tom Mannion Landscape Design; 185 top left: Kappel & Phelps; 185 bottom left: Huettl-Thuilot Associates; 185 right: Oehme, van Sweden & Associates; 187 top: Kappel & Phelps; 187 bottom: Arentz Landscape Architects; 188–189: Scott Colombo Designs; 191: Monika Hellwegen and Azul Cobb, Carlotta from Paradise; 192: Lighting design by Outdoor Illumination; 193 top right: Rosemary Wells, Viridian Landscape Architecture; 193 bottom right: Bud Stuckey; 194 top left: Scott Brinitzer Design Associates; 194 middle left: Tom Mannion Landscape Design; 194 bottom left: Lara Dutto, D-Cubed; 195: Jeffrey Gordon Smith; 196: Jon Buerk, J. Buerk Landscape/Maintenance; 197 top left: P.O.P.S. Landscaping; 197 top right: Dean Riddle; 197 bottom: Bernard Trainor + Associates; 198 left: Mark Marcinik, Greenmeadow Architects; Elliot Goliger, Artisans Landscape; 198 right: Rober Glazier, Hill Glazier Architects, and Andrew Glazier, Wild West Gardens; 199 left: Scott Huston, Columbine Design; 199 right: Tom Wilhite; 200–201: Tara Dillard Garden Design; 202: Michael Manneh and Stefan Offermann; 203 top: Cevan Forristt Landscape Design; 203 bottom: the Fockele Garden company; 204 top: Craig Bergmann Landscape Design; 204 bottom: Bernard Trainor + Associates; 205: David Yakish; 207: Shari Bashin-Sullivan and Richard Sullivan; 208: Terry Mulrooney, Admiral Green Landscaping; 210: Iron Age Designs; 211 right: Vanessa Kuemmerle, Vee Horticulture; Bluejay Feldman, Blue Ridge Landscape Co.; 212: Raymond Jungles Inc.; 213 right: Windsmith Design; 214: Kappel & Phelps; 215 top: Mark Marcinik, Greenmeadow Architects; Elliot Goliger, Artisans Landscape; 215 middle: Wes Brittenham; 216: Landscape Design: Christy Ten Eyck, Ten Eyck Landscape Architects; Design: McCoy and Simon Architects; 217: Mark Licht, Clemens & Associates; 218: Sydney Eddison; 220: Craig Bergmann Landscape Design.

Index

Special Thanks

We would like to thank the designers, architects, and builders who contributed to this book, and the homeowners who graciously allowed us to photograph their backyards. Kimberley Burch, Bill Stephens, and Spencer Toy of *Sunset* deserve a huge thank you for their help in coordinating the photography. Special thanks to Ben Marks of Sunset Books, and Sally Reilly of Time Inc.

Sunset guides you to a fabulous home – inside and out

Bathrooms — A *Sunset* Design Guide

Backyards — A *Sunset* Design Guide

Kitchens — A *Sunset* Design Guide

Patio & Stone — A *Sunset* Design Guide

Home Decor — A *Sunset* Design Guide
inspiration + expert advice

Design with Color — A *Sunset* Design Guide
inspiration + expert advice — Easy Color Schemes that Work

Sunset's all-new Design Guides have everything you need to plan — and create — the home of your dreams. Each book includes advice from top professionals and hundreds of illustrative photos. With an emphasis on green building materials and techniques, this entire series will inspire ideas both inside and outside of your home.